AF255884

COUNTRY SKIES

Prayerful Bible Meditations for Morning & Evening

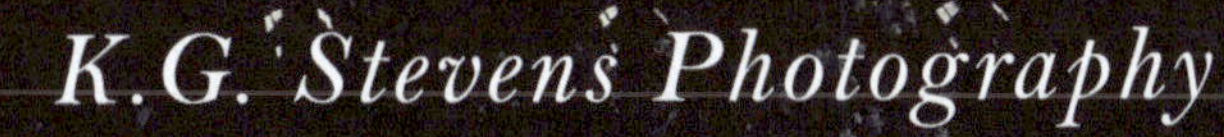

COUNTRY SKIES

Prayerful Bible Meditations for
Morning & Evening

K.G. Stevens Photography

Country Skies
Prayerful Bible Meditations for Morning and Evening
Copyright © 2019 by Santa Rosa Press

Project Manager and Team Coordinator Mary Cindell Lynn Pilapil
Cover design by Albert Cesar Compay
Interior design by Vanz Edmar Mariano

This edition is published by Santa Rosa Press
For more information, contact publisher@santarosapress.net

First Edition
ISBN 978-0-9890405-8-7 (Hardcover)
ISBN 978-0-9890405-9-4 (Paperback)

Publisher's Cataloging-in-Publication Data

Names: Stevens, K.G. Photography
Title: Country Skies: Prayerful Bible Meditations For Morning And Evening / Photography by K.G. Stevens Photography.
Description: Thousand Oaks, CA: Santa Rosa Press, 2019.
Identifiers: LCCN 2019949452 | ISBN 978-0-9890405-8-7 (Hardcover) | 978-0-9890405-9-4 (Paperback)
Subjects: LCSH Bible--Meditations. | Meditations. | Sky--Pictorial works. | Devotional literature. | BISAC RELIGION / Biblical Meditations / General | RELIGION / Christian Life / Inspirational. | PHOTOGRAPHY / Individual Photographers / Artists' Books
Classification: LCC BV4832.3 .S74 2019 | DDC 242--dc23

Book Design: Raket Creatives
Printed and published in the United States of America

A portion of

proceeds from this

book will be

donated to

to families in need.

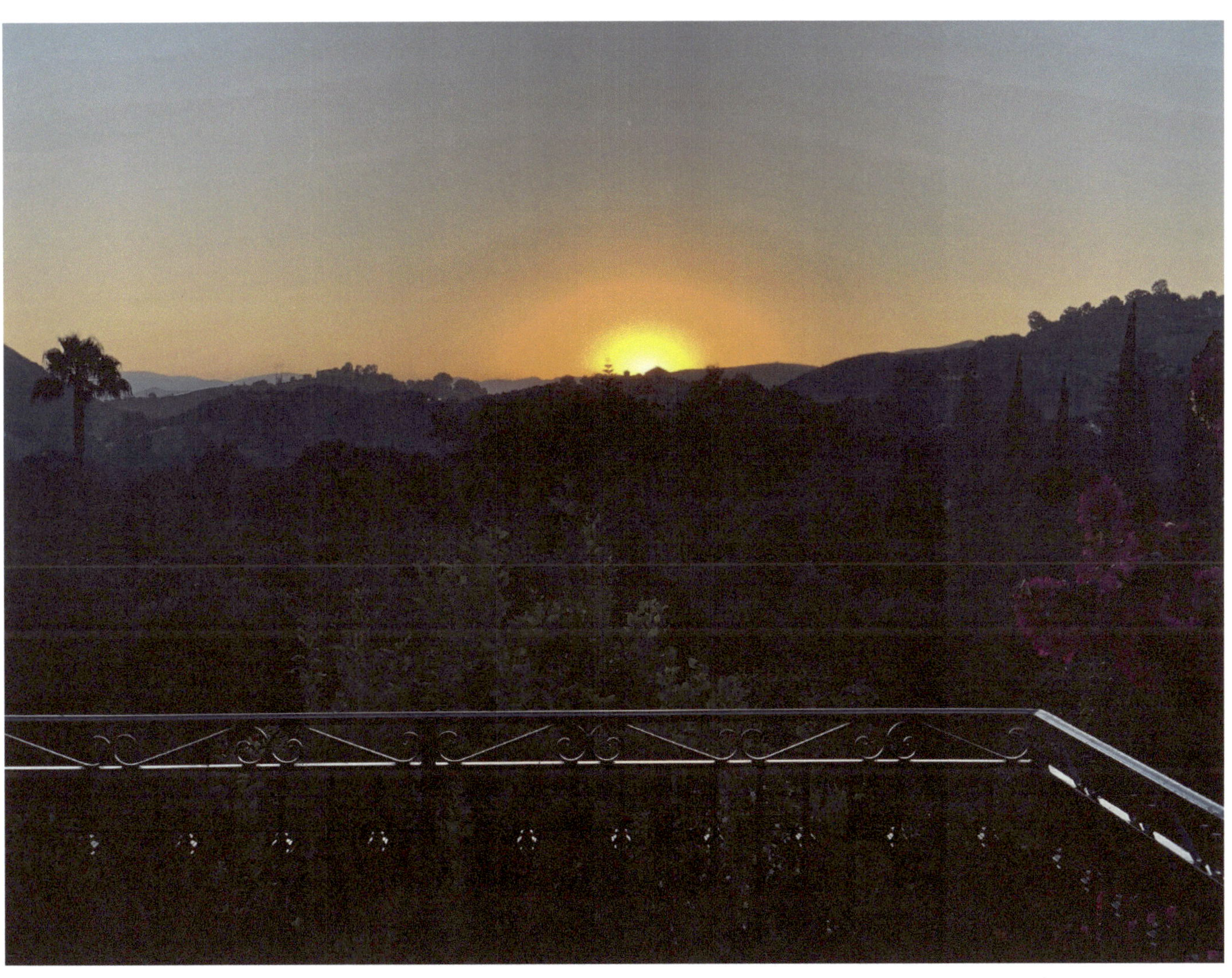

The whole EARTH is filled with AWE at YOUR

WONDERS;

where morning DAWNS, where evening FADES,

YOU call FORTH songs of joy.

—PSALM 65:8

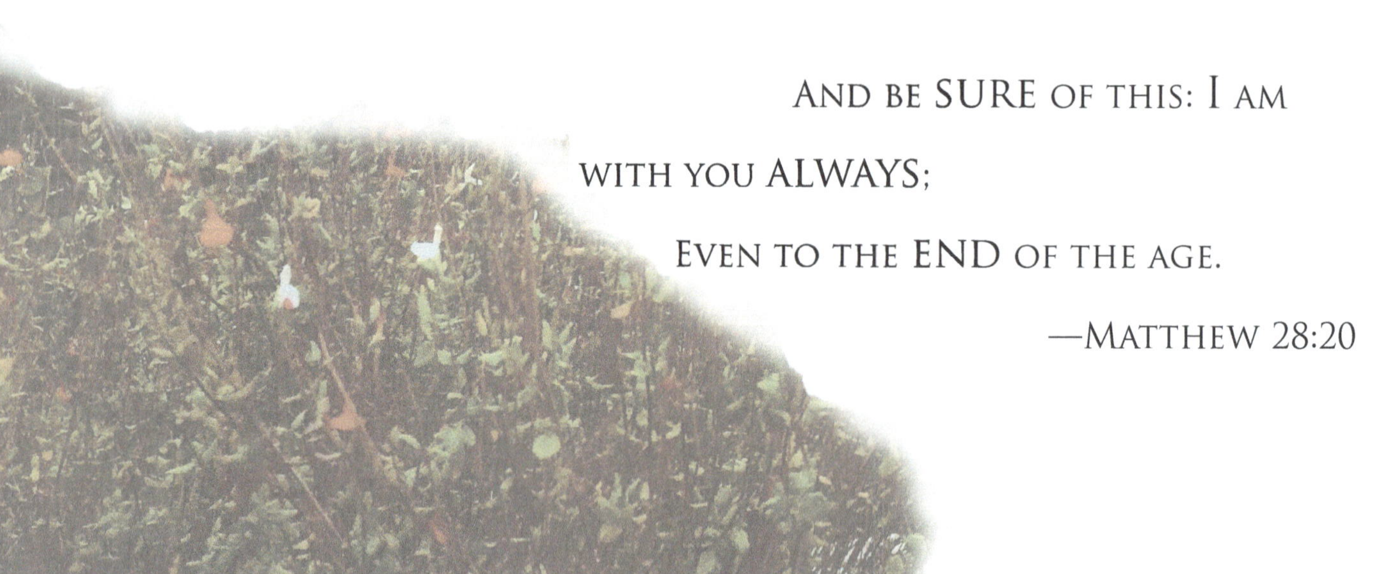

AND be SURE of this: I am

with you ALWAYS;

Even to the END of the age.

—MATTHEW 28:20

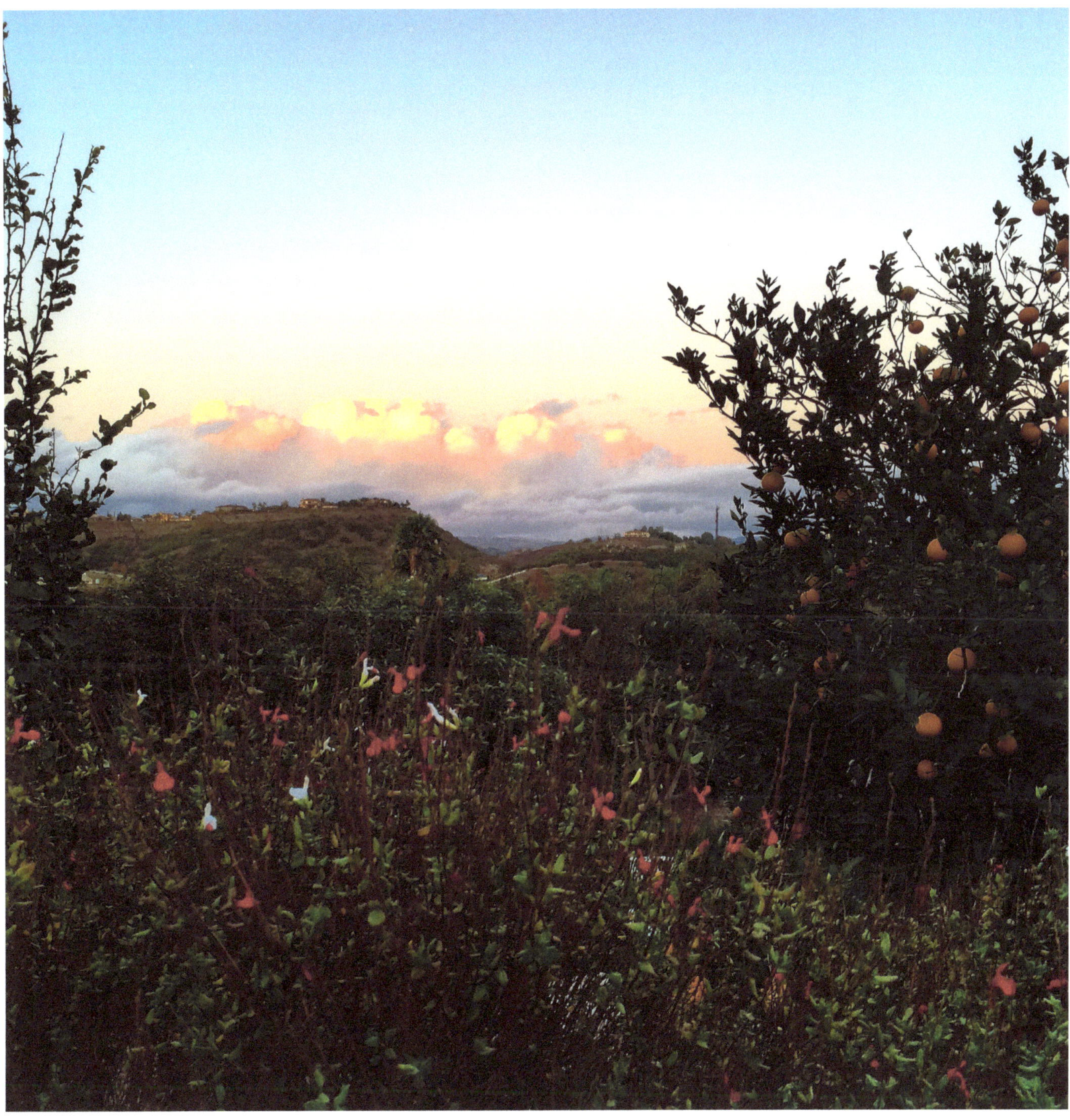

BROTHERS AND SISTERS,

WHATEVER IS TRUE,

WHATEVER IS NOBLE,

WHATEVER IS RIGHT,

WHATEVER IS PURE,

WHATEVER IS LOVELY,

WHATEVER IS ADMIRABLE,

—IF ANYTHING IS

EXCELLENT

OR PRAISEWORTHY—

THINK ABOUT SUCH

THINGS.

—PHILIPPIANS 4:8

THE LORD IS MY SHEPHERD;
I SHALL NOT WANT.

—PSALM 23:1

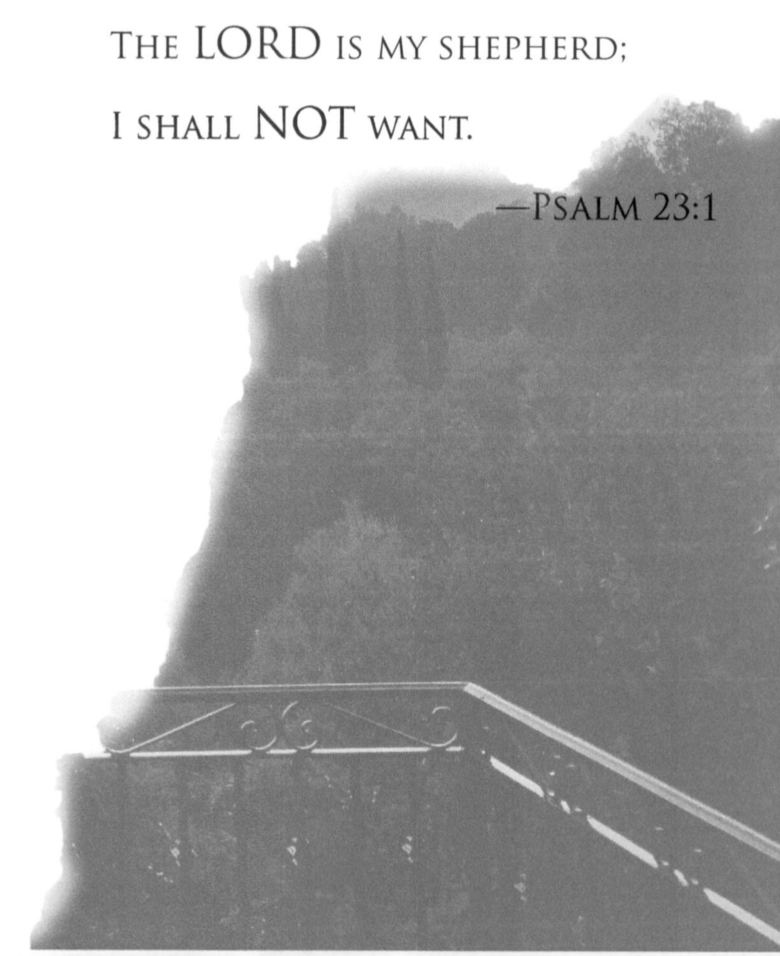

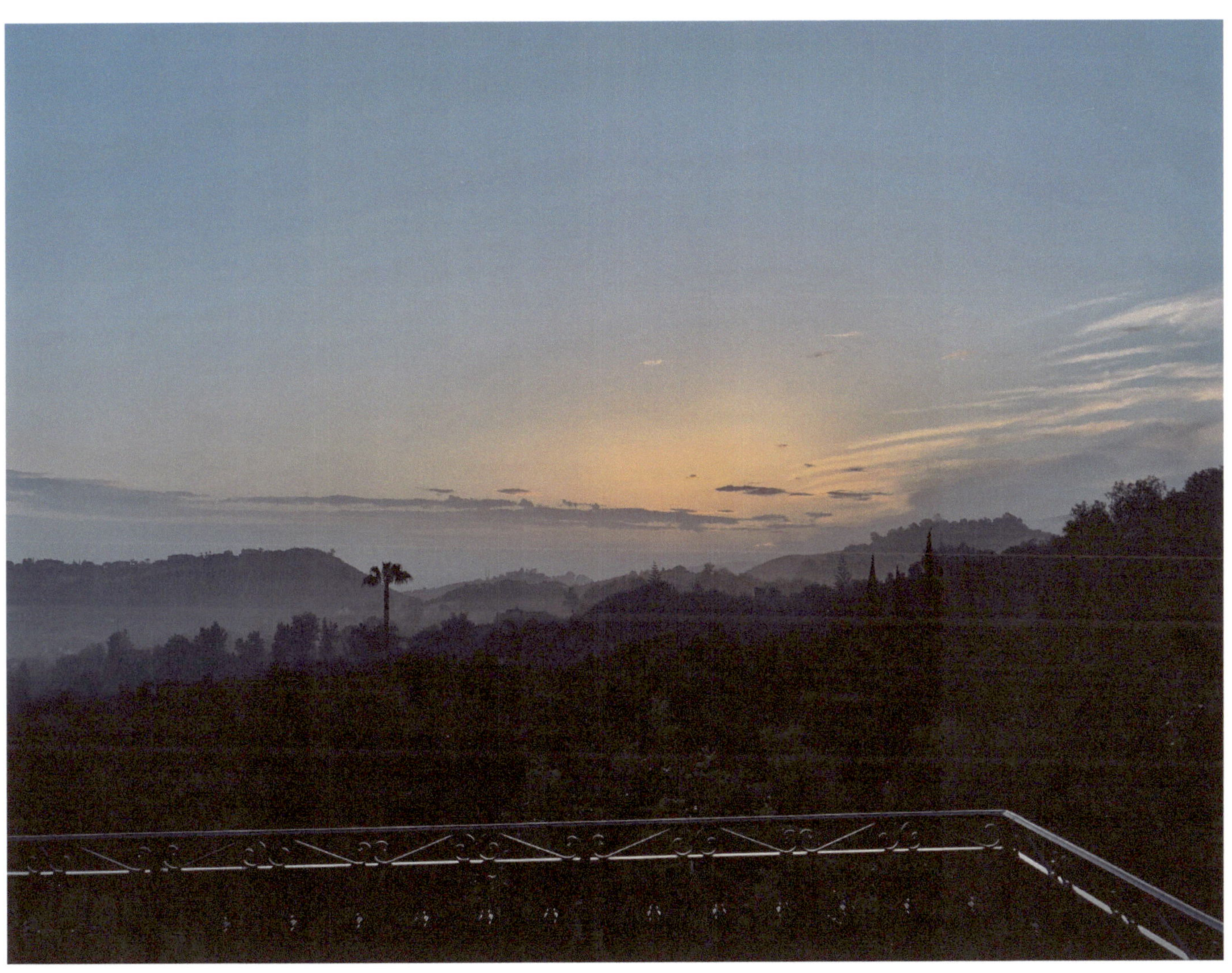

JESUS LOOKED AT THEM AND SAID,

"WITH MAN THIS IS IMPOSSIBLE, BUT

WITH GOD ALL THINGS ARE POSSIBLE."

—MATTHEW 19:26

IF GOD IS FOR US,

WHO CAN BE AGAINST US?

—ROMANS 8:31

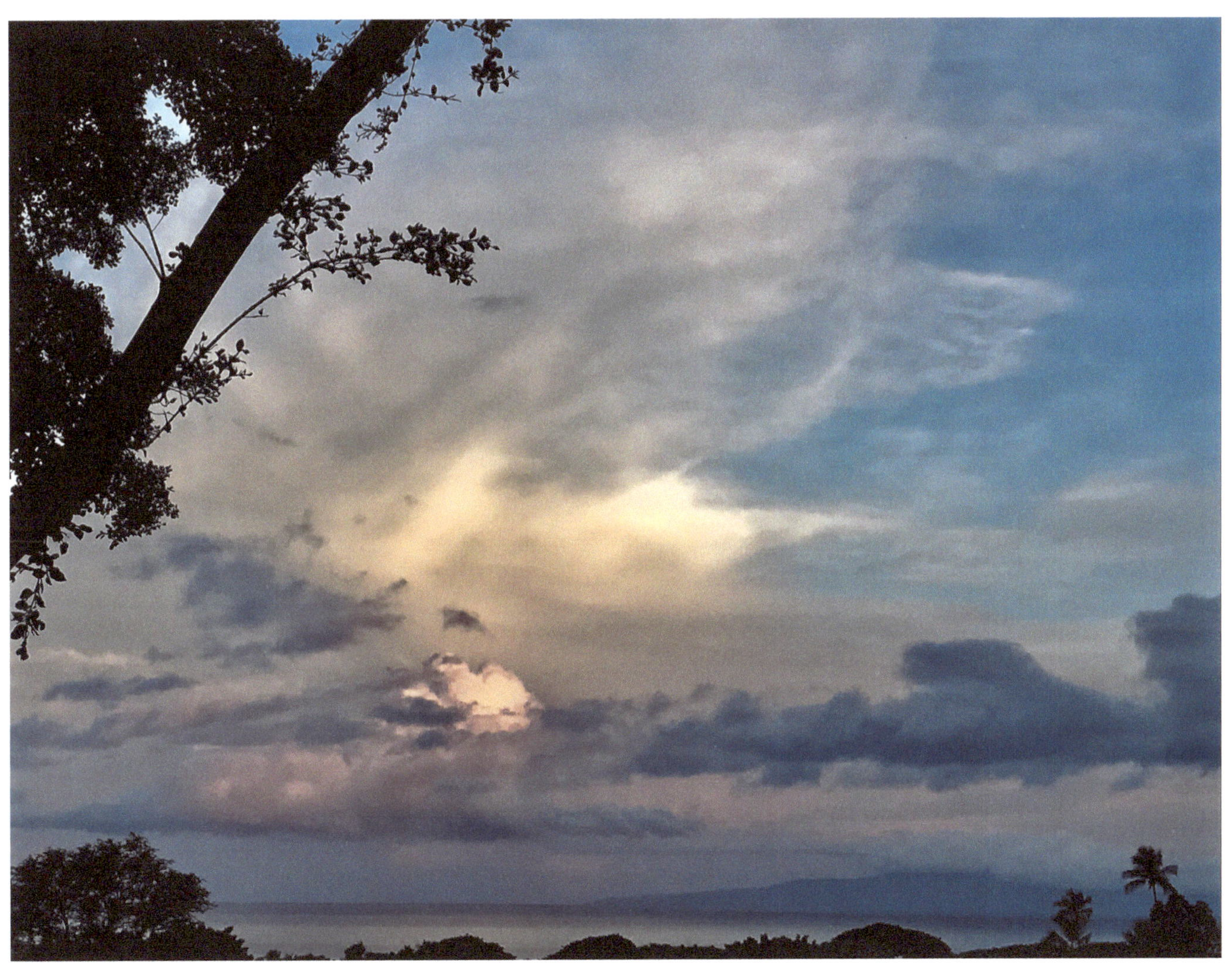

Be STRONG and COURAGEOUS,
Do not be AFRAID; do not be
DISCOURAGED, for the LORD your
GOD will be WITH YOU wherever
you GO.

—Joshua 1:9

Therefore shall a MAN leave his FATHER and
his MOTHER, and shall JOIN to his wife:
and they shall be ONE flesh.

—Genesis 2:24

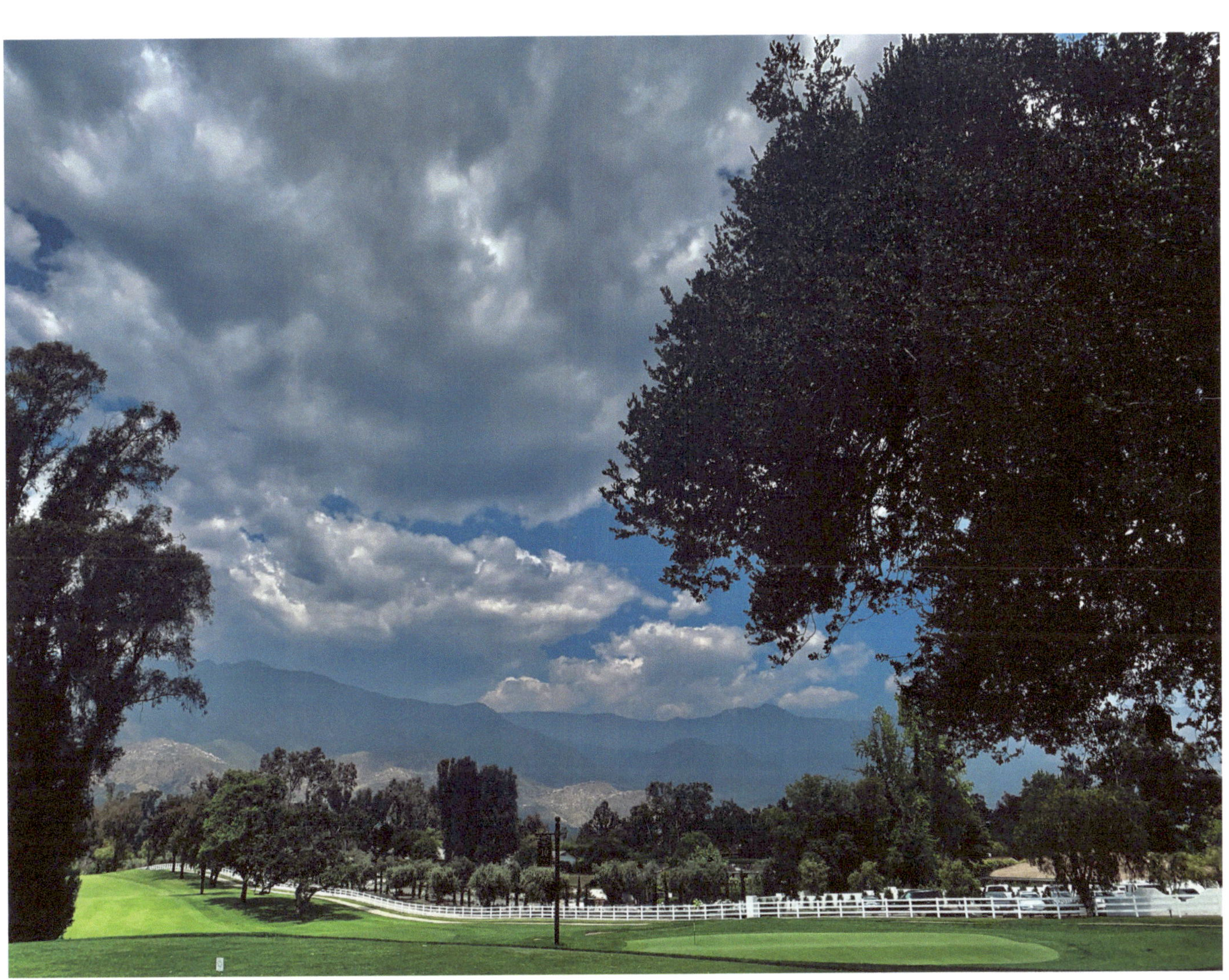

Let ALL that you DO be

done in LOVE.

—I Corinthians 16:14

You will SEEK *ME* and

FIND *ME* when you SEEK

ME with ALL your HEART.

—Jeremiah 29:13

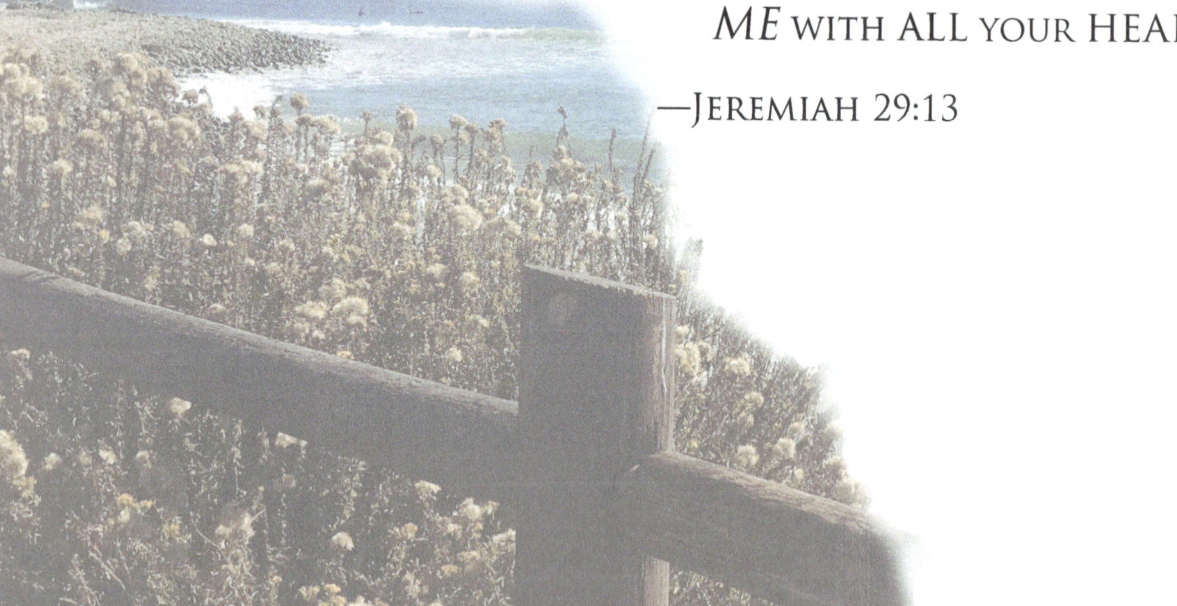

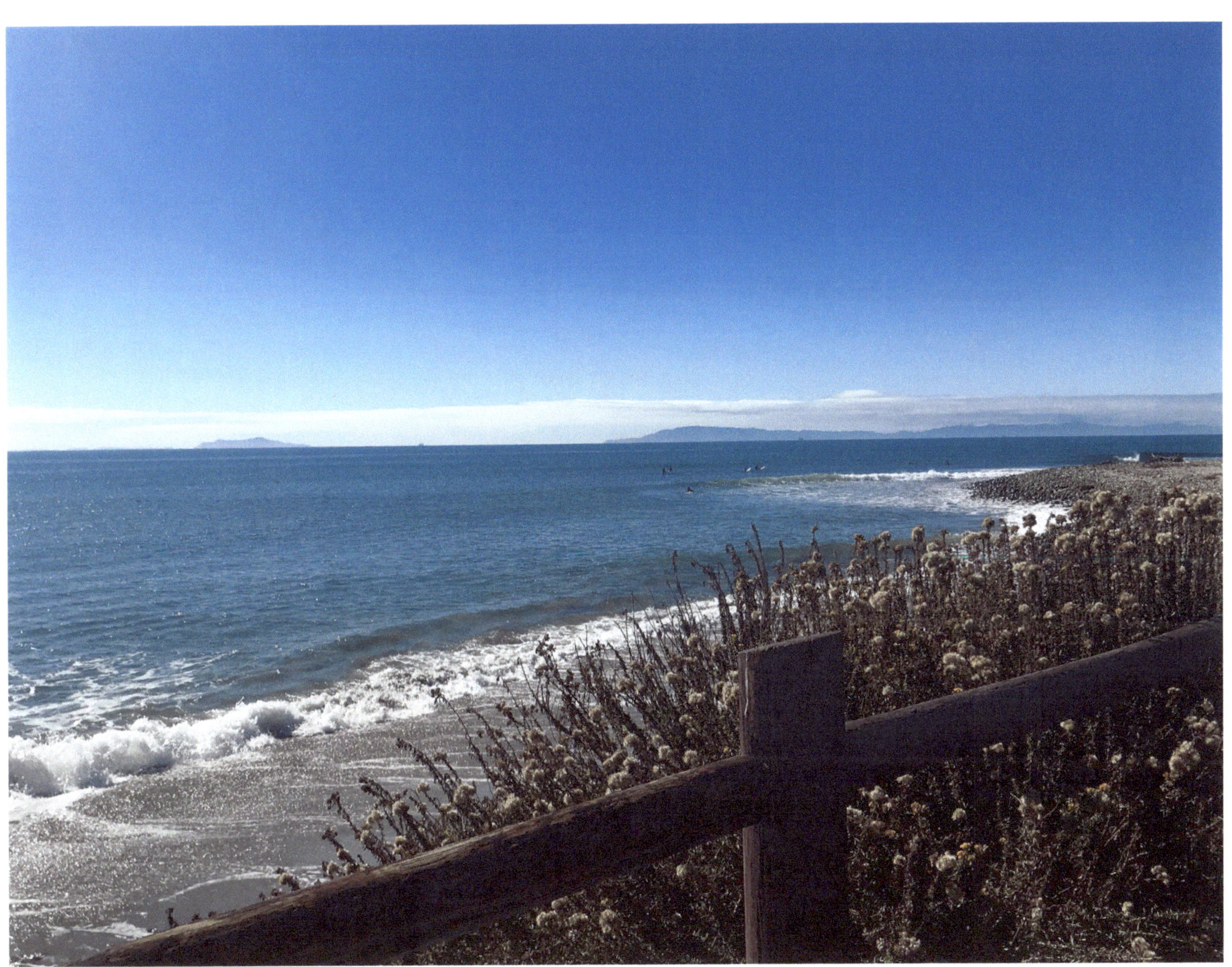

CAST your cares on the LORD and

HE will SUSTAIN you; HE will never

let the RIGHTEOUS be shaken.

—Psalm 55:22

FOR GOD so loved the world that HE gave HIS one

and only Son, that whoever believes in HIM should

NOT PERISH BUT HAVE ETERNAL LIFE.

—John 3:16

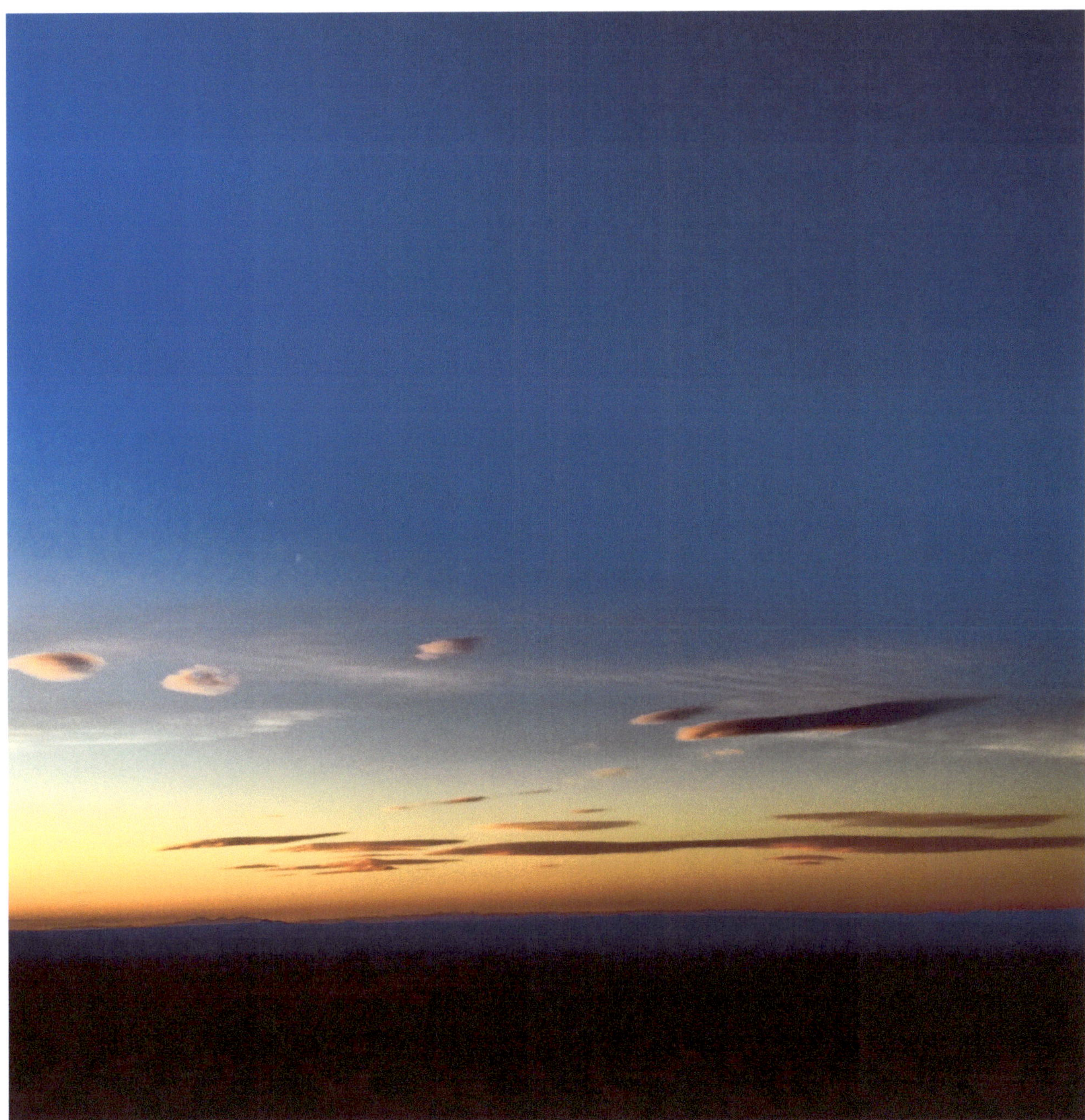

Look to the LORD and HIS
STRENGTH;
seek HIS face ALWAYS.

—1 Chronicles 16:11

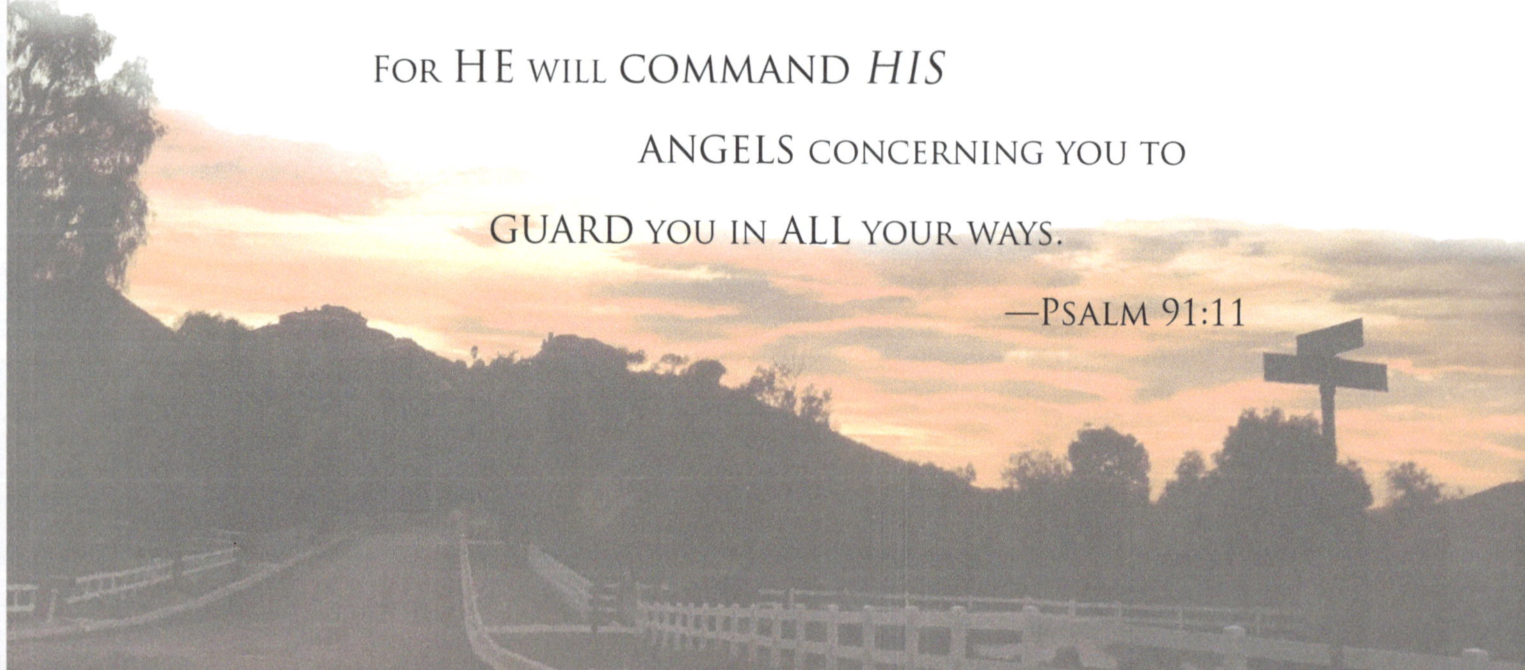

For HE will COMMAND *HIS*
ANGELS concerning you to
GUARD you in ALL your ways.

—Psalm 91:11

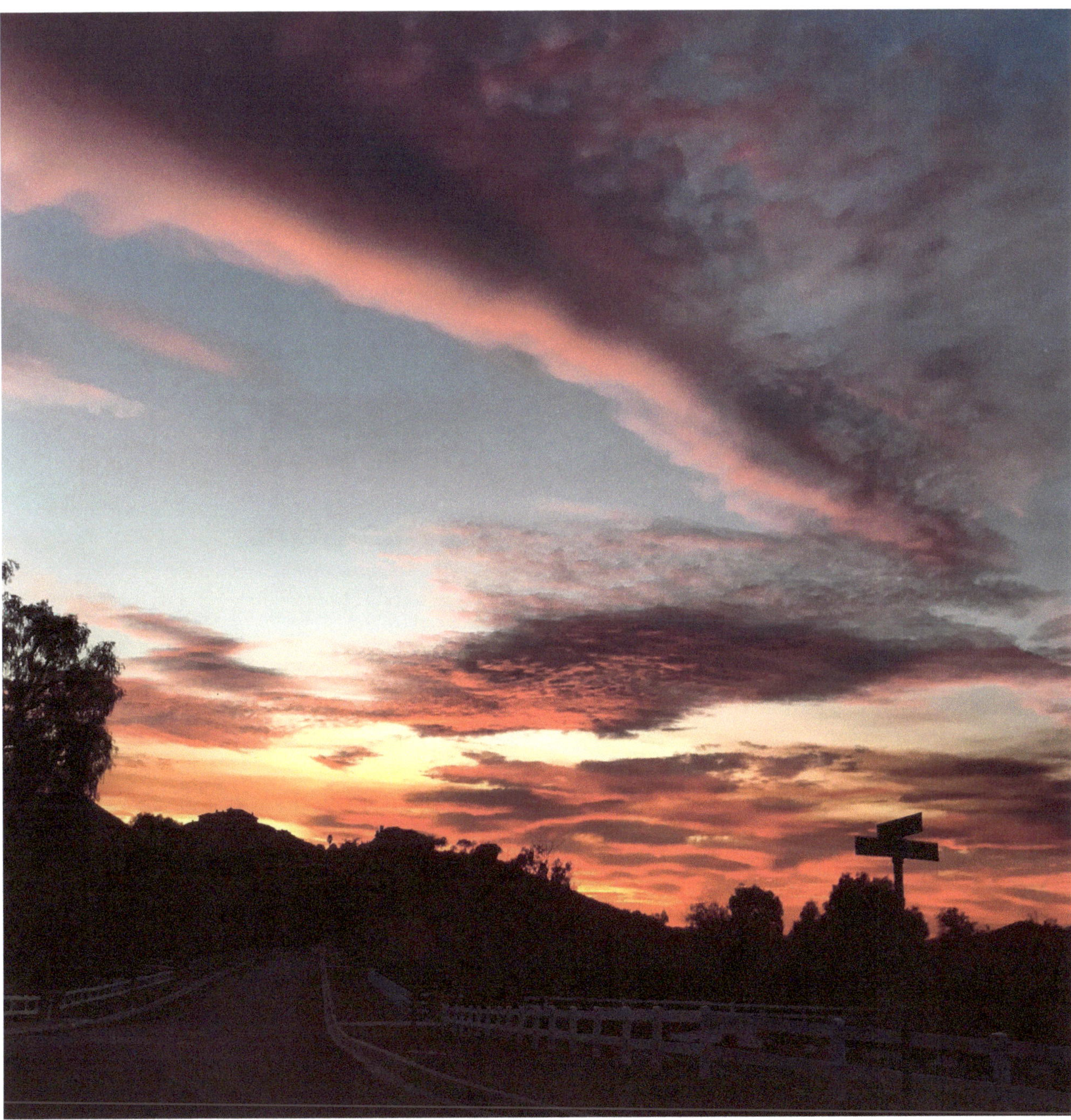

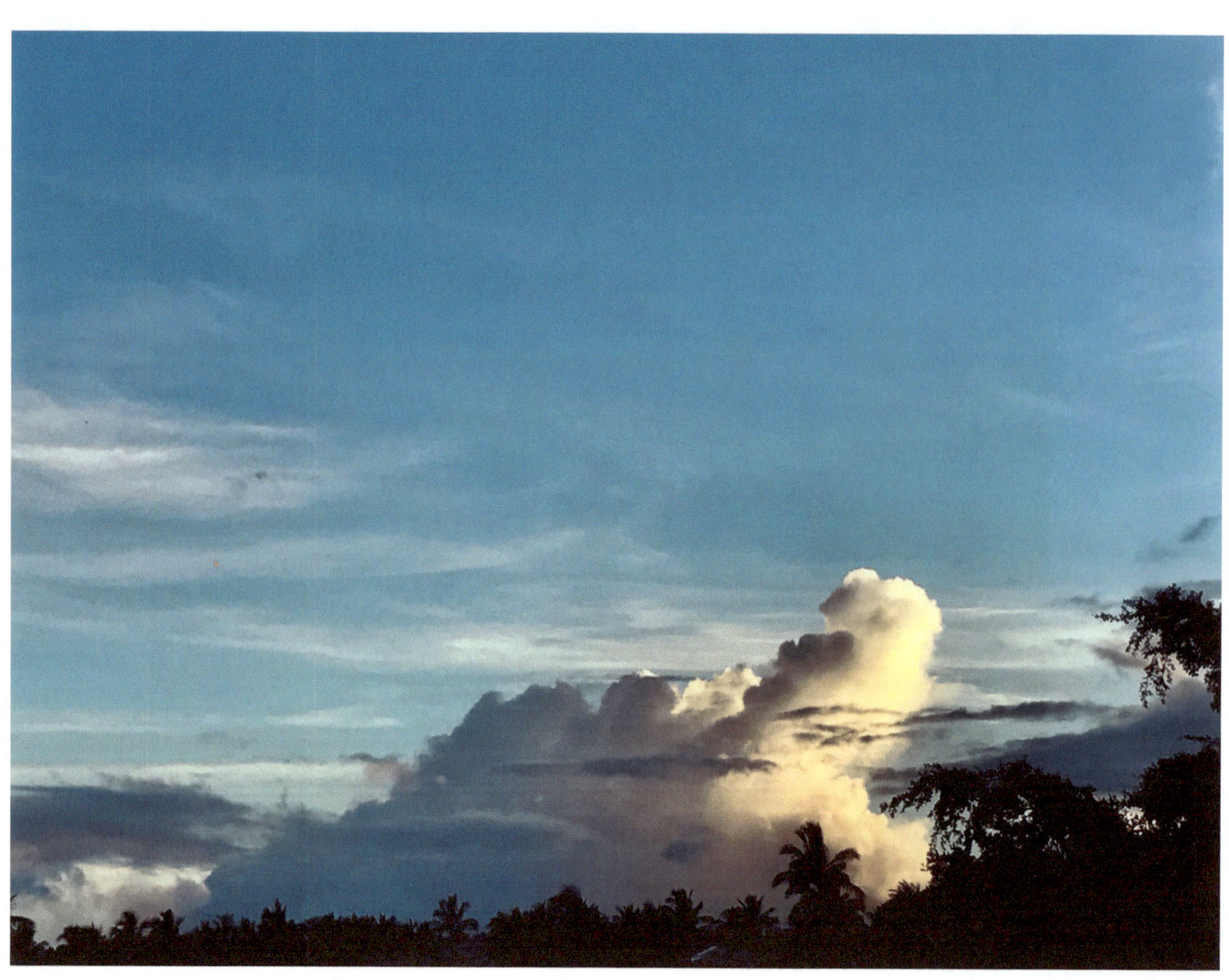

ARISE, for *this* matter *is* your *RESPONSIBILITY*. WE ALSO *ARE* WITH YOU. BE OF GOOD COURAGE, AND DO *IT*.

—EZRA 10:4

LOVE BEARS ALL THINGS, BELIEVES ALL THINGS, HOPES ALL THINGS, ENDURES ALL THINGS.

—I CORINTHIANS 13:7

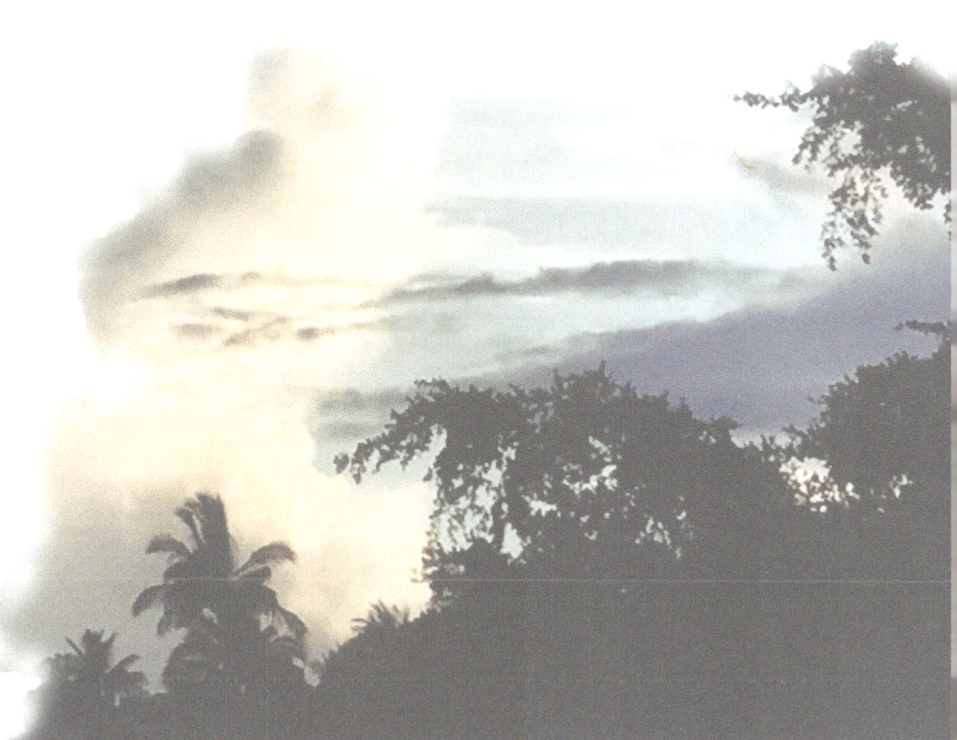

Therefore HE says:

"AWAKE, you who SLEEP,

ARISE from the DEAD,

AND CHRIST will give you LIGHT."

—Ephesians 5:14

Even to your OLD age, *I am* HE,

And even to gray hairs I will CARRY *you*!

I have MADE, and I will BEAR;

Even I will CARRY, and will DELIVER *you*.

—Isaiah 46:4

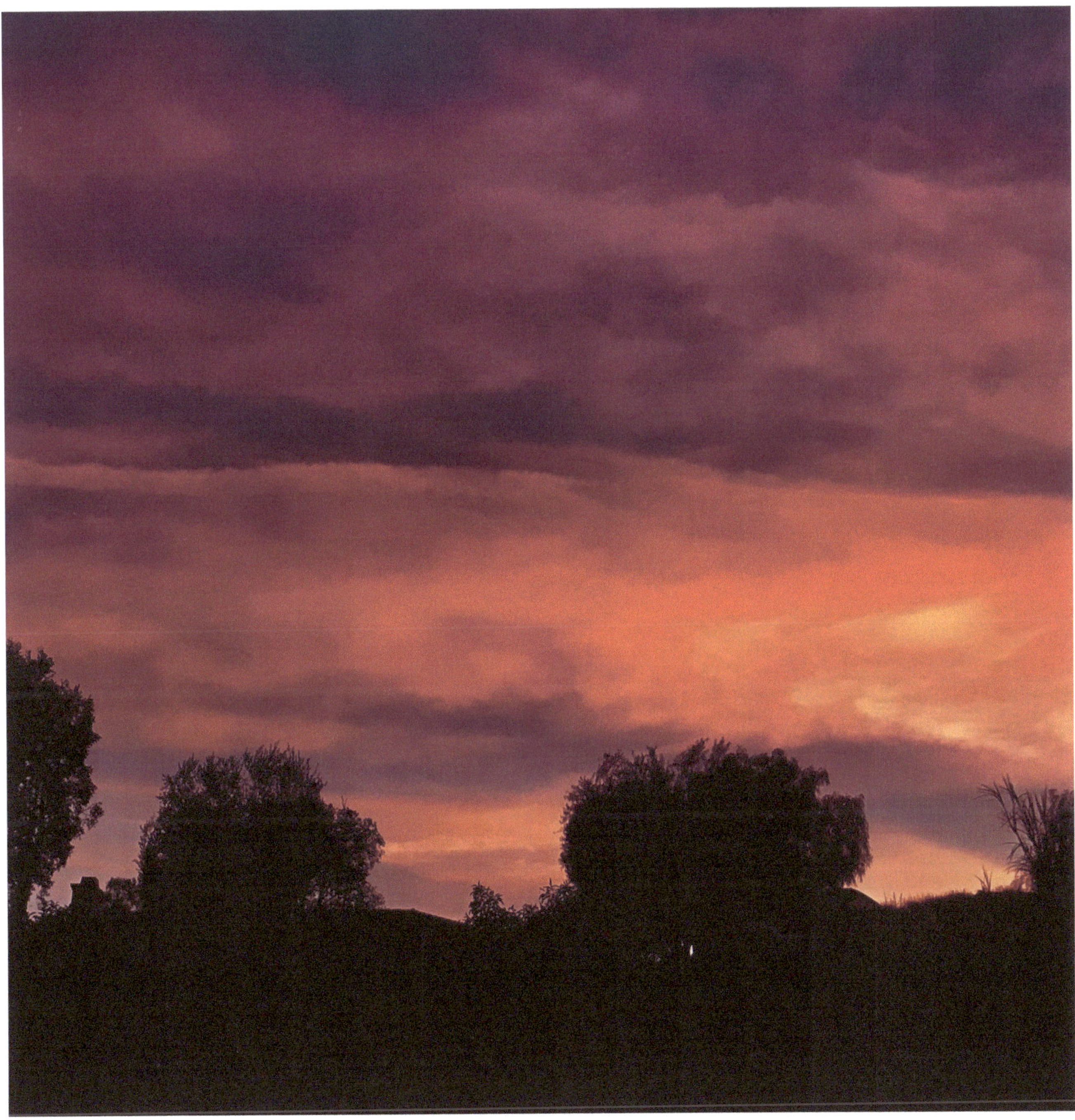

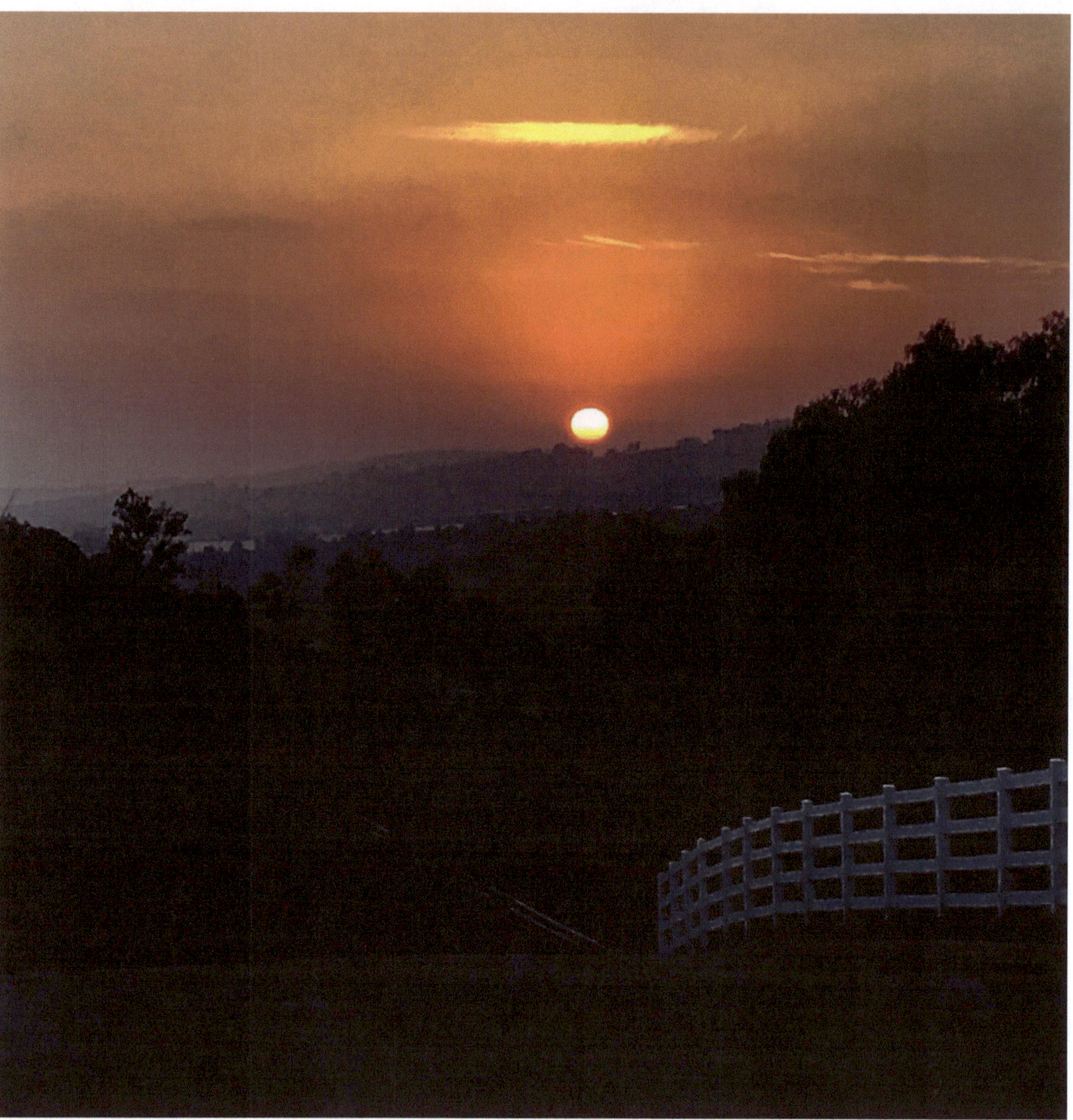

Greater LOVE has no one than
this, than to lay down one's LIFE
for his FRIENDS.
—John 15:13

JESUS said to him, "I am the WAY, the
TRUTH, and the LIFE. No one comes to
the FATHER except through ME."
—John 14:6

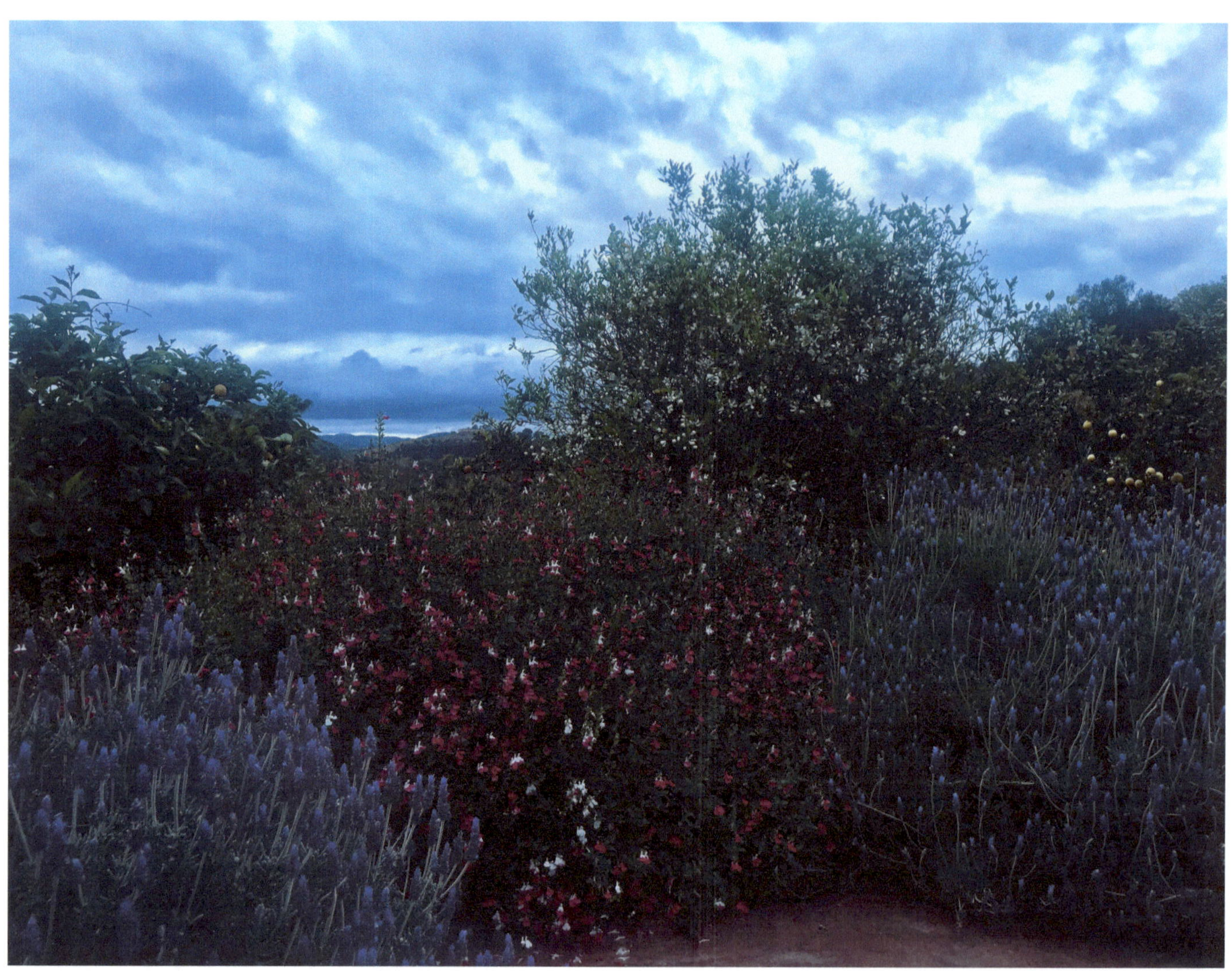

Let the WORDS of my mouth and the MEDITATION of my

heart,

Be ACCEPTABLE in YOUR sight,

o LORD, my strength and my Redeemer.

—Psalm 19:14

Show me *YOUR* ways, o LORD:

Teach me YOUR paths.

Lead me in *YOUR* truth and teach me,

For YOU are the GOD of my SALVATION;

on YOU I wait all the day.

—Psalm 25

Those who are WISE shall shine

Like the brightness of the FIRMAMENT,

And those who turn many to RIGHTEOUSNESS Like

the STARS forever and ever.

—Daniel 12:3

The LORD is my rock and my fortress and my

DELIVERER,

My GOD, my ROCK, in whom I take refuge,

My shield and the horn of my SALVATION, my

STRONGHOLD.

—Psalm 18:2

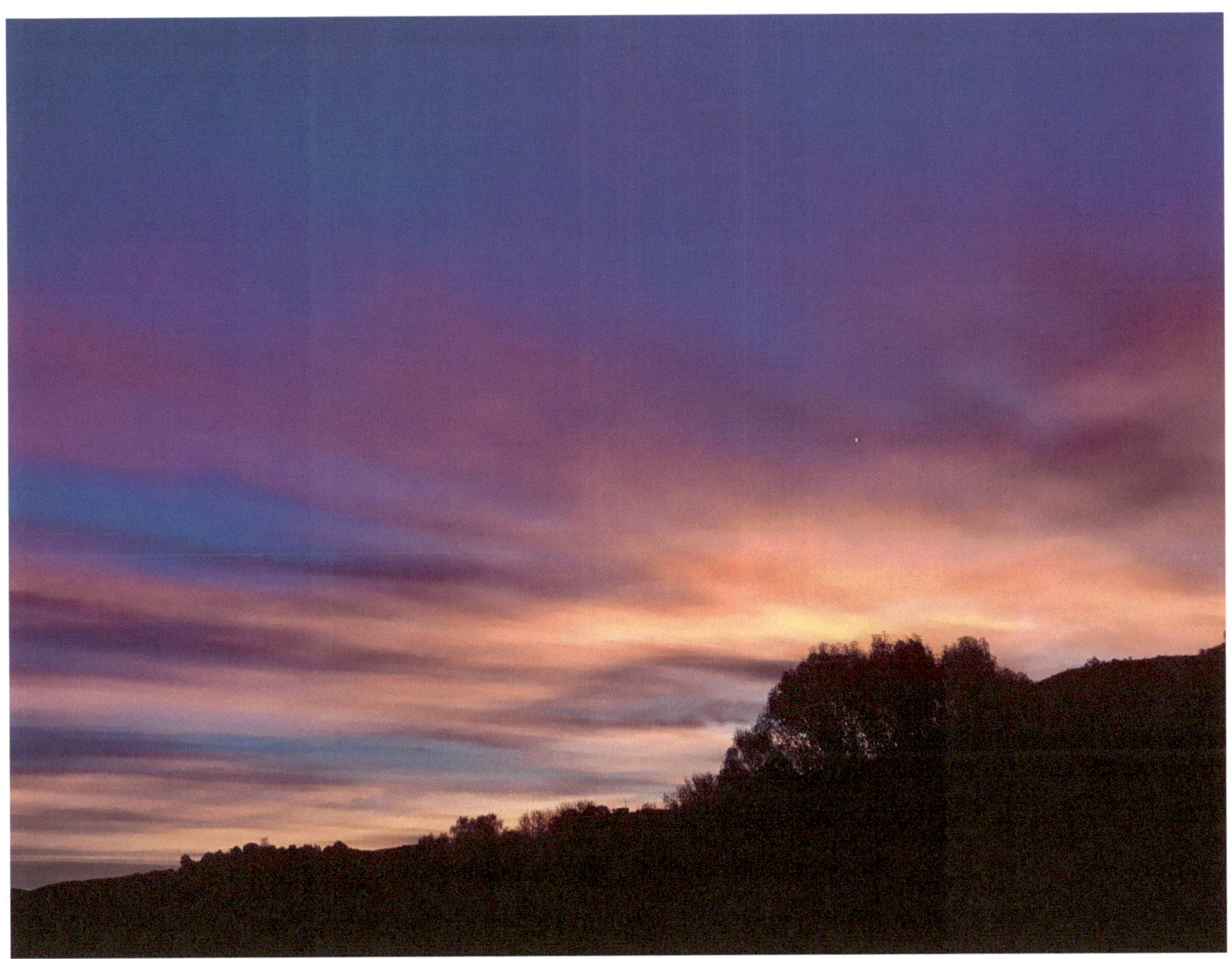

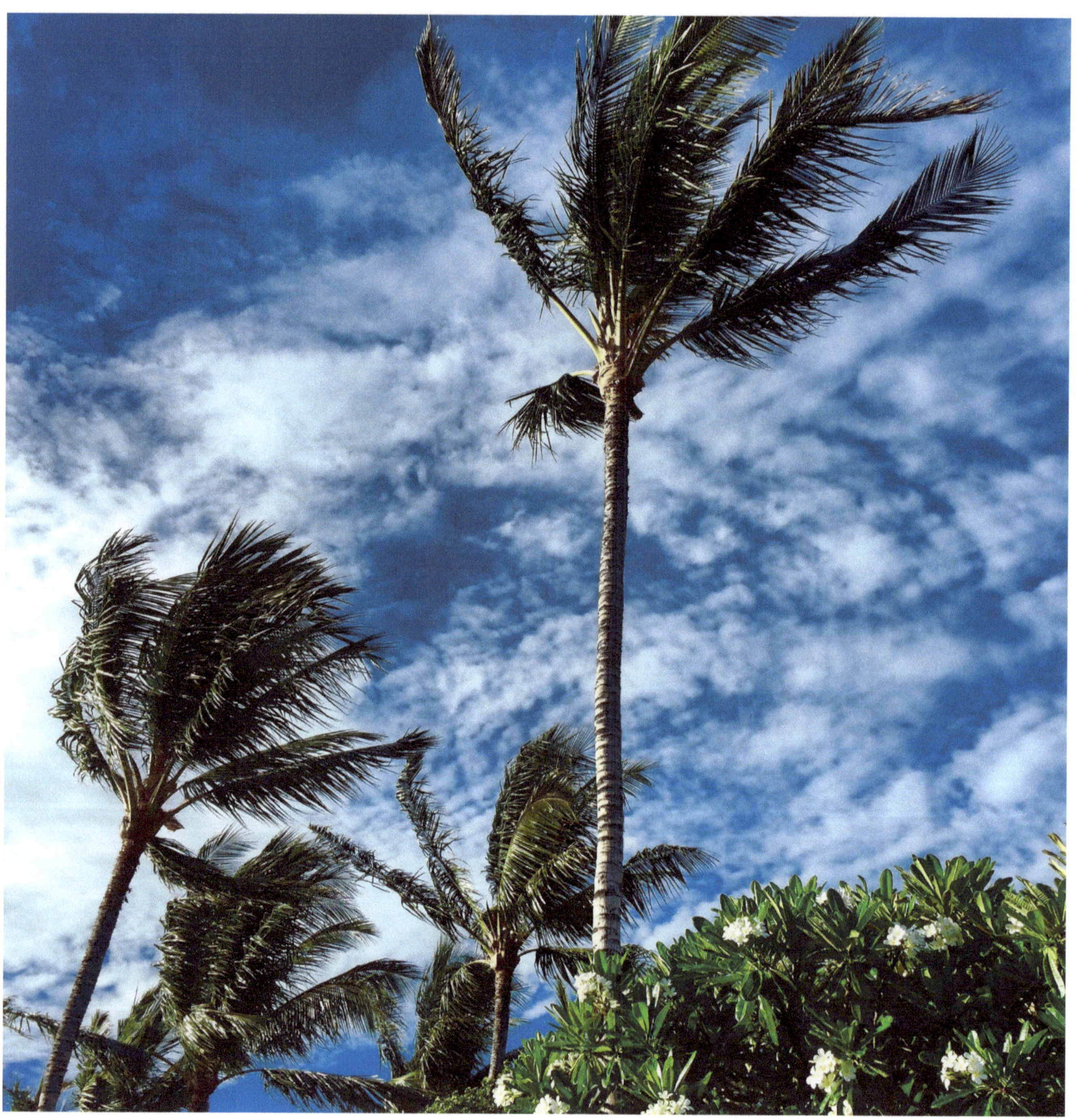

Commit your WAY to the LORD,

Trust also in HIM,

And HE shall bring *it* to pass.

—Psalm 37:5

For it is BETTER, if it is the WILL of GOD, to suffer

for doing GOOD than doing evil.

—1 Peter 3:17

For *HIS* ANGER *is but* for a moment,

HIS favor *is* for LIFE;

WEEPING may endure for a night,

But joy *comes* in the MORNING.

—Psalm 30:5

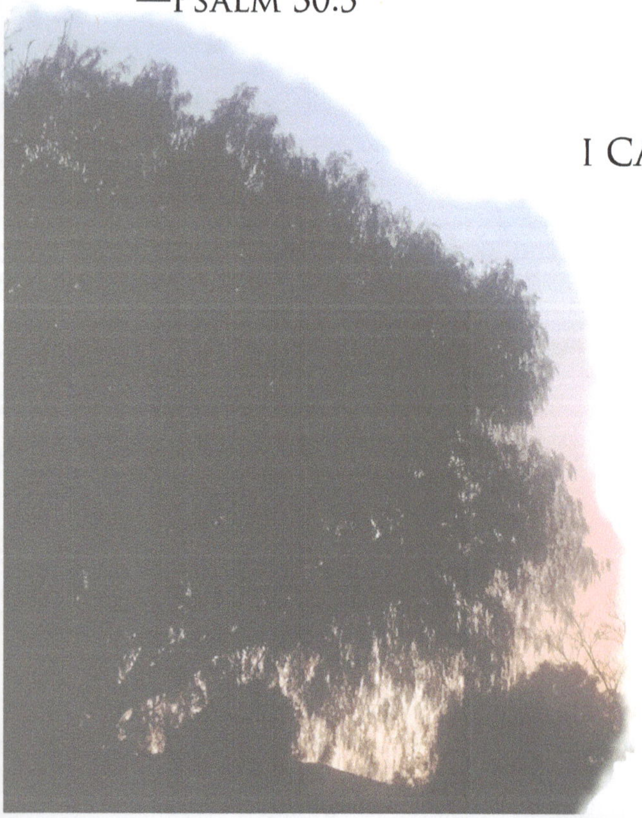

I CAN do all things through CHRIST who

strengthens ME.

—Philippians 4:13

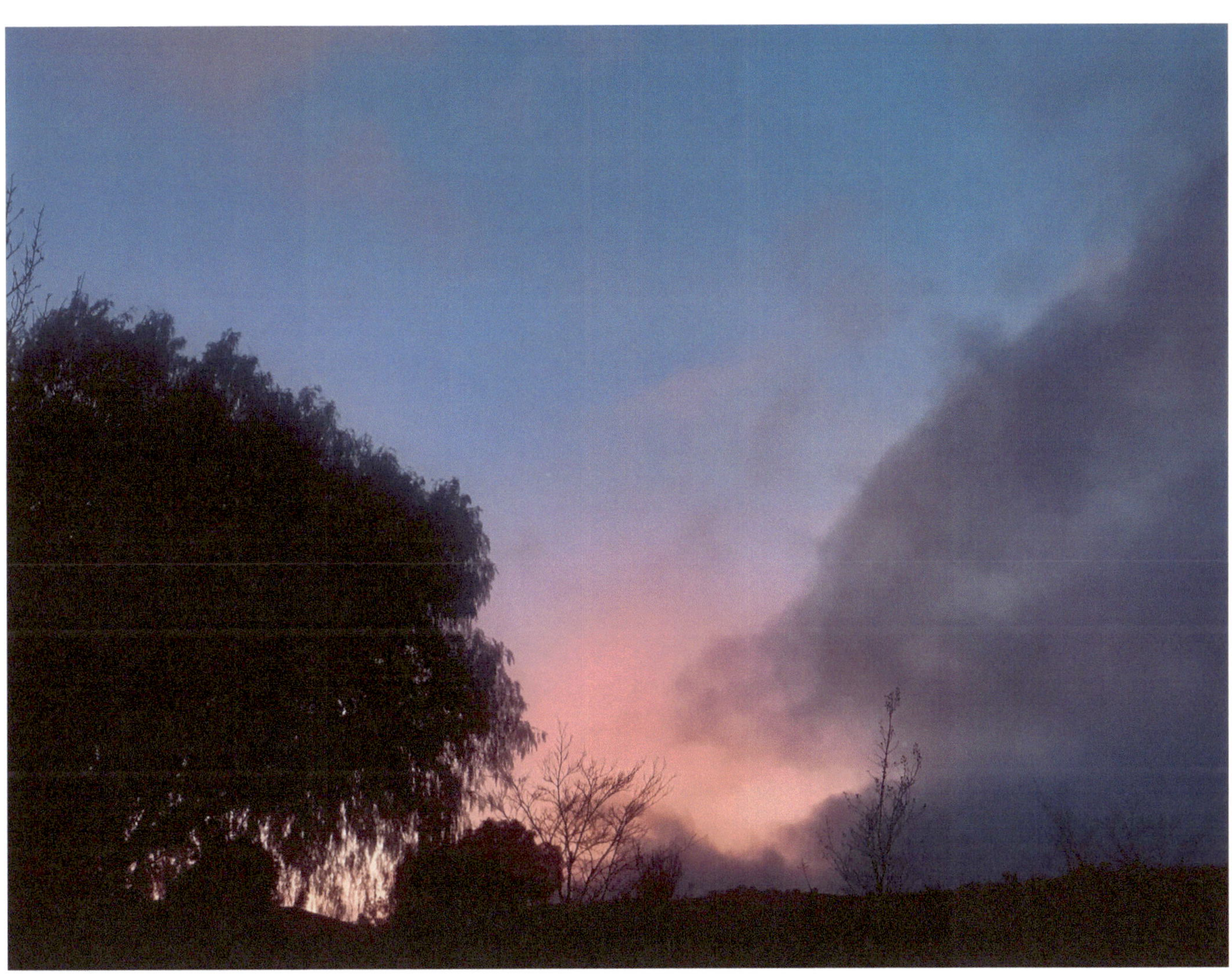

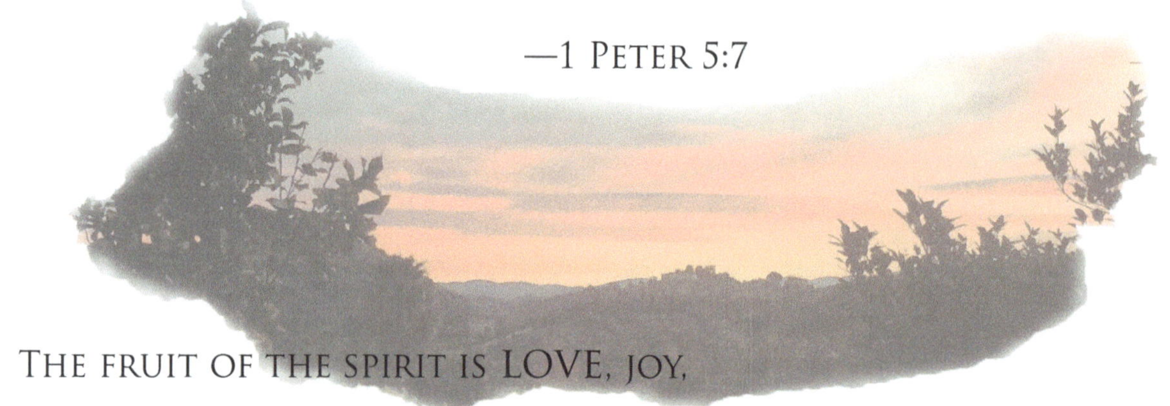

Cast all your ANXIETY upon HIM,

for HE cares for you.

—1 Peter 5:7

The fruit of the spirit is LOVE, joy,

peace, long-suffering, KINDNESS,

GOODNESS, faithfulness,

gentleness, self-control.

—Galatians 5:22-23

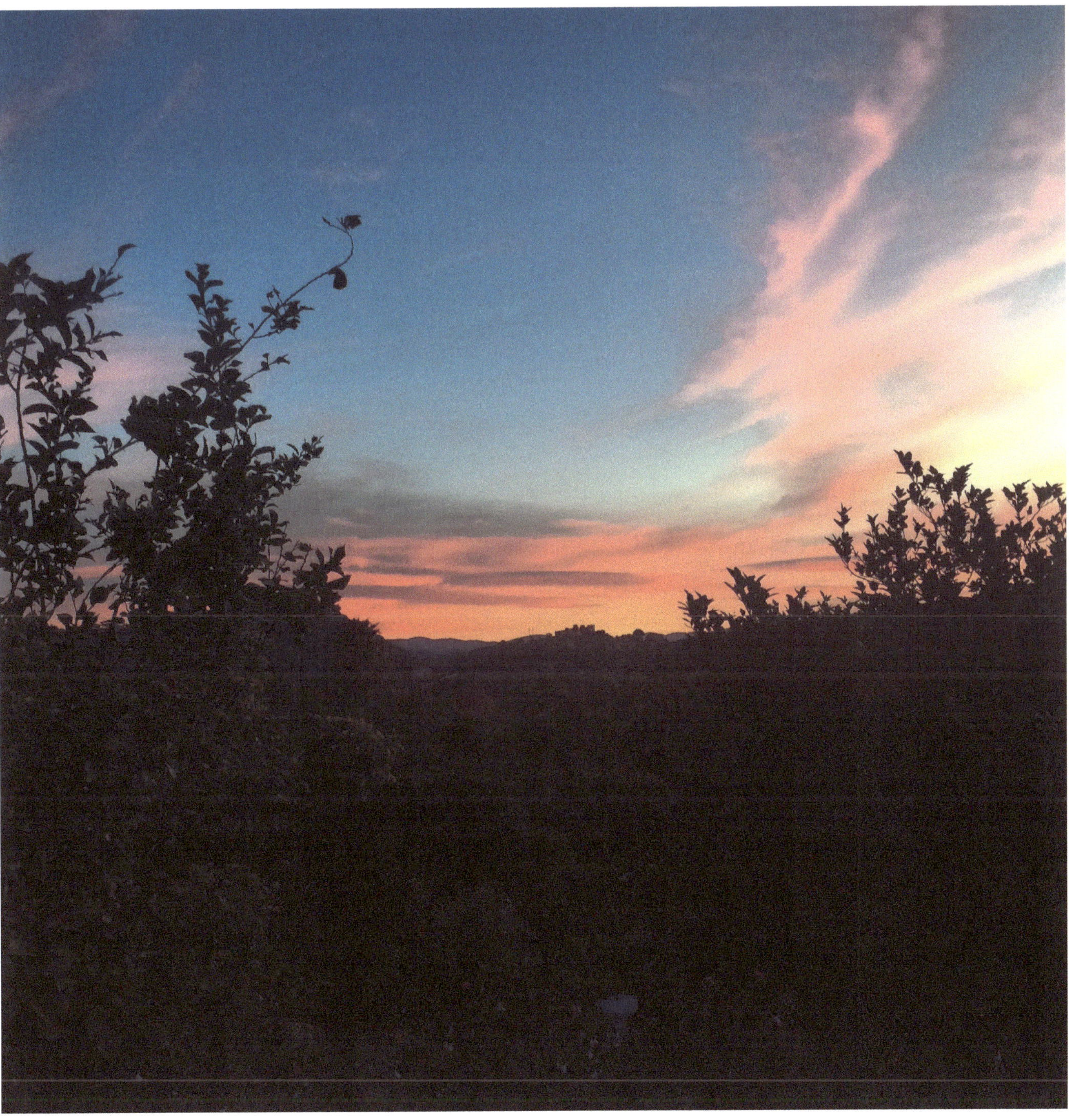

Oh, taste and SEE that the LORD is
good;
Blessed is the man *who* TRUSTS in
HIM.

—Psalm 34:8

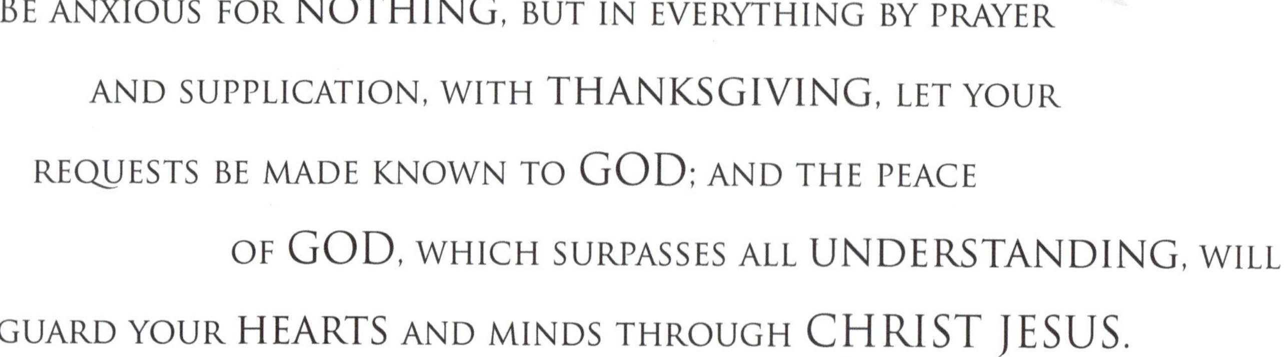

Be anxious for NOTHING, but in everything by prayer
and supplication, with THANKSGIVING, let your
requests be made known to GOD; and the peace
of GOD, which surpasses all UNDERSTANDING, will
guard your HEARTS and minds through CHRIST JESUS.

—Philippians 4:6-7

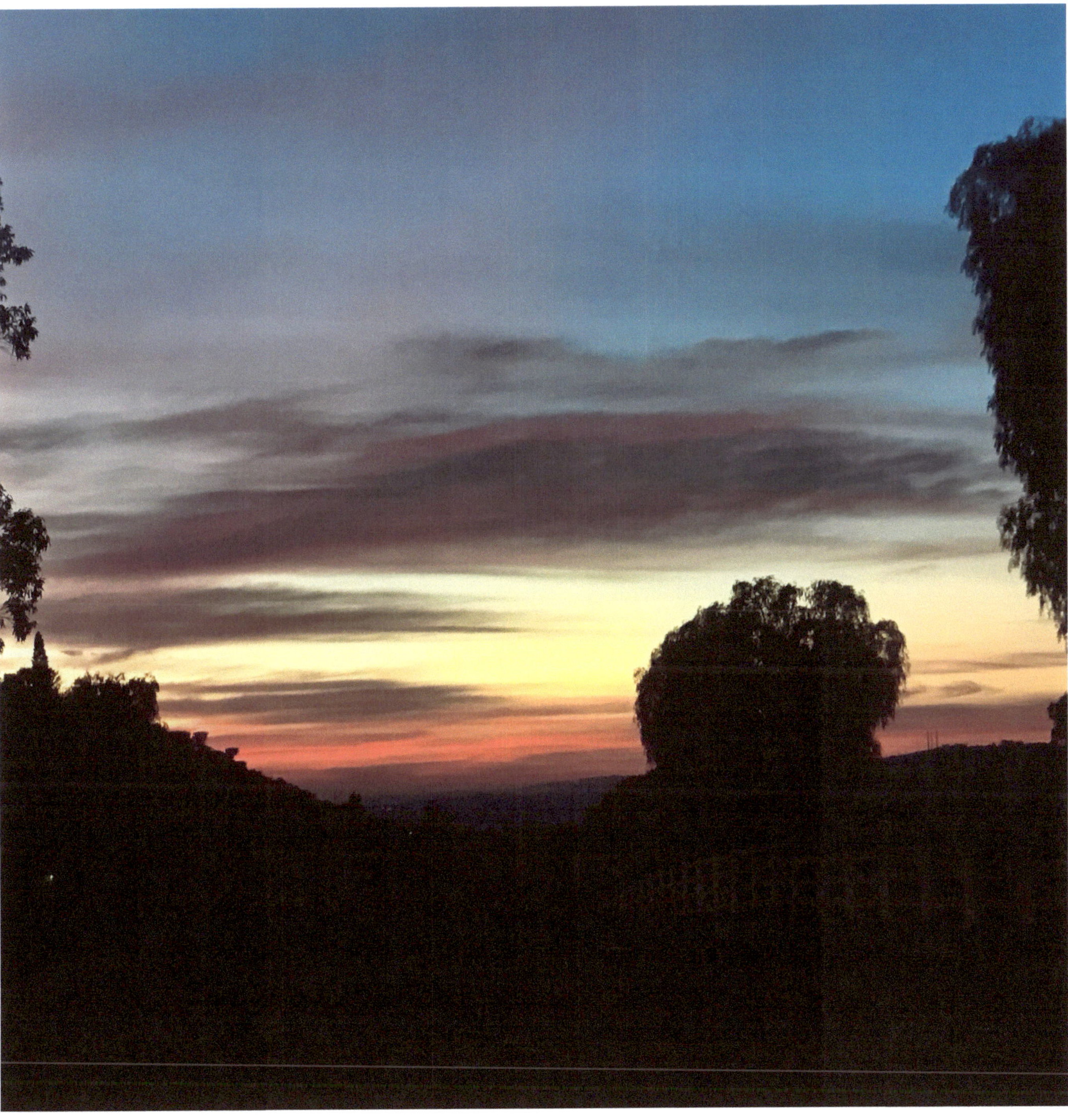

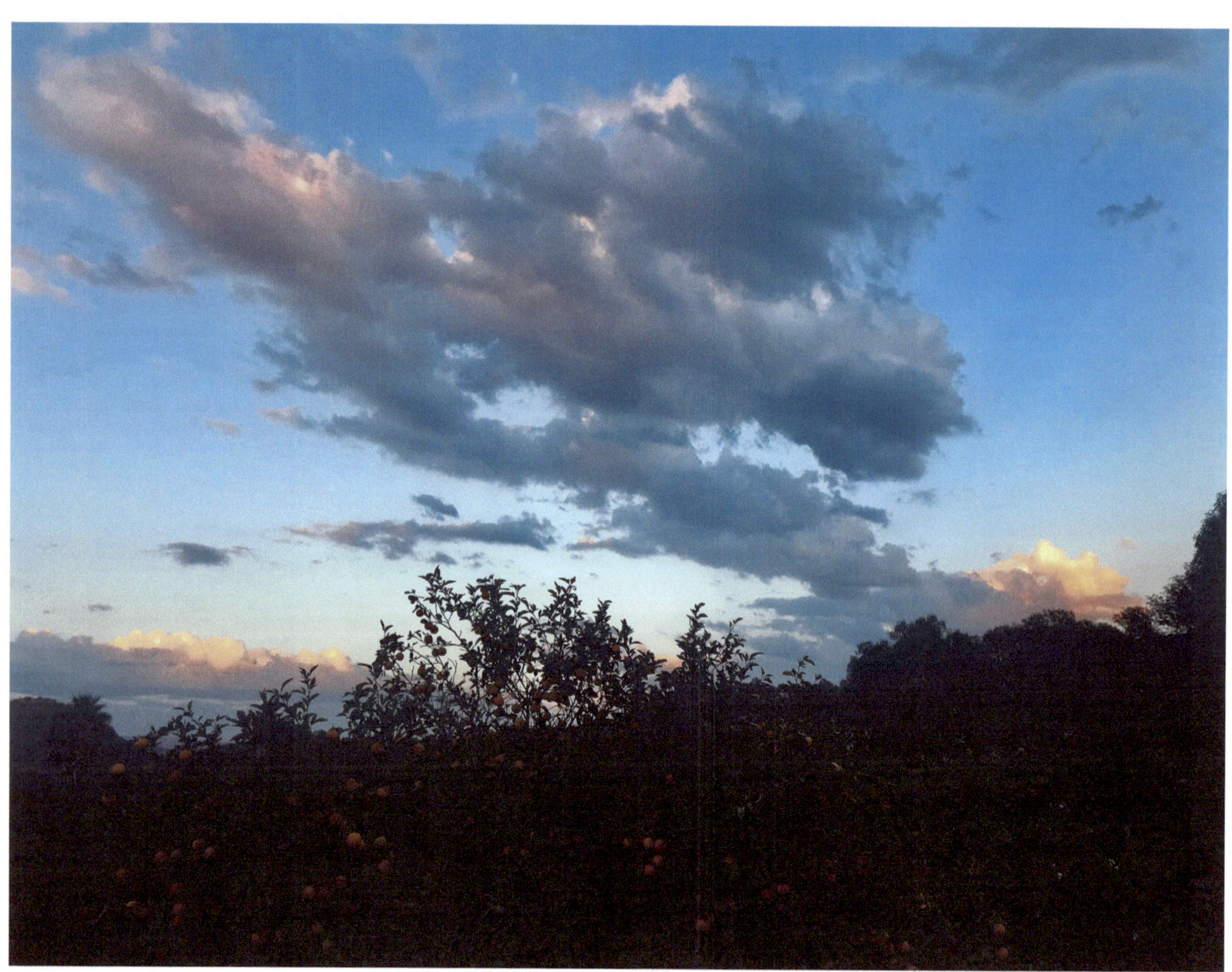

AND WE KNOW THAT ALL THINGS WORK
TOGETHER FOR GOOD TO THOSE WHO LOVE
GOD, TO THOSE WHO ARE THE CALLED
ACCORDING TO *HIS* PURPOSE.

—ROMANS 8:28

COME TO ME,
ALL YOU WHO LABOR AND ARE HEAVY LADEN,
AND I WILL GIVE YOU REST.

—MATTHEW 11:28

And WHATEVER you do, do it HEARTILY, as to the LORD and not to men.

—Colossians 3:23

Do not FEAR, little flock, for it is your FATHER'S good PLEASURE to give you the KINGDOM.

—Luke 12:32

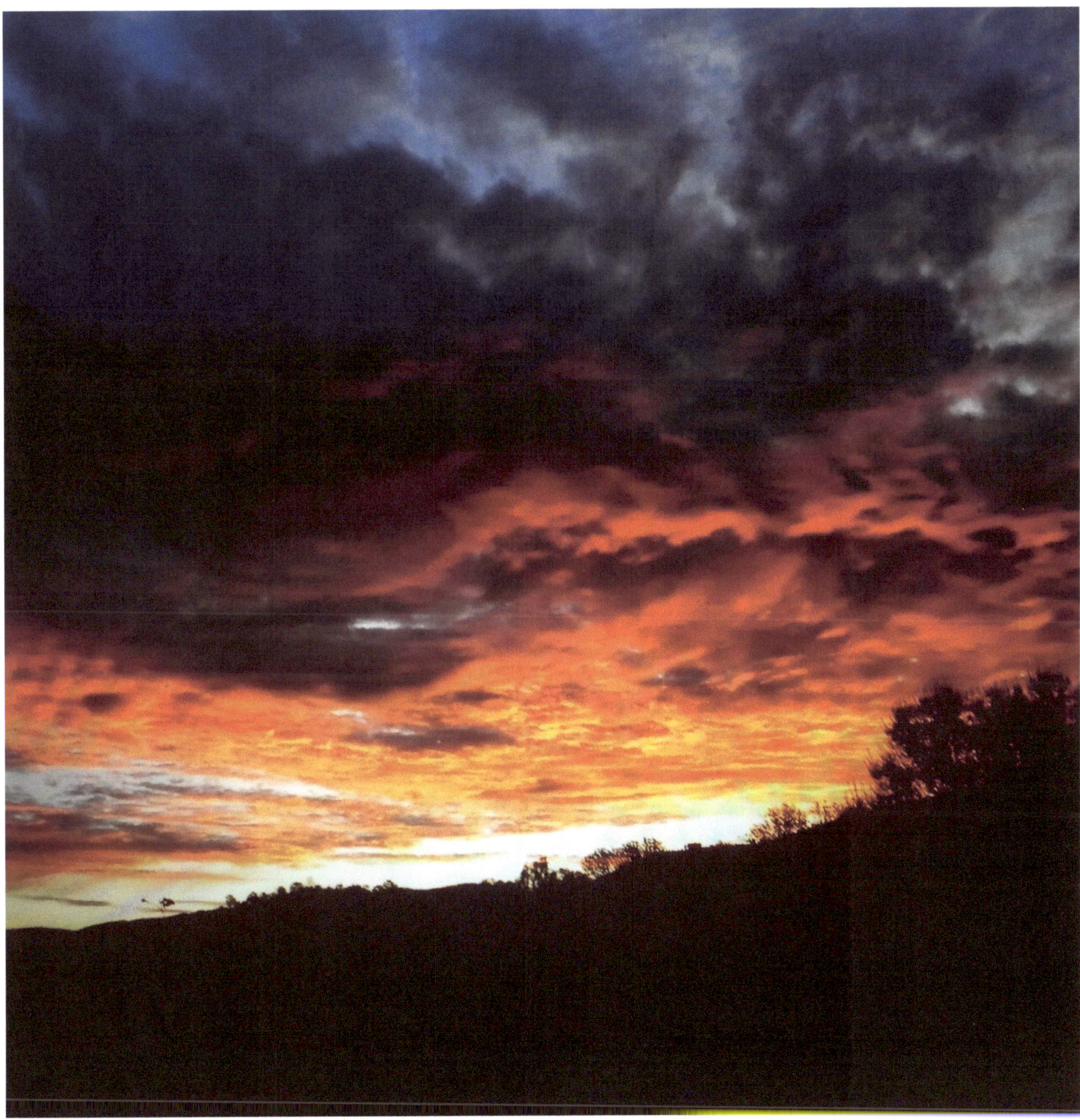

Trust in the LORD with all your HEART,

And LEAN not on your own understanding;

In all your ways ACKNOWLEDGE *HIM*,

And HE shall direct your PATHS.

—Proverbs 3:5-6

PRAY without ceasing, in everything

give THANKS; for this is the will of GOD in

CHRIST JESUS for YOU.

—1 Thessalonians 5:17-18

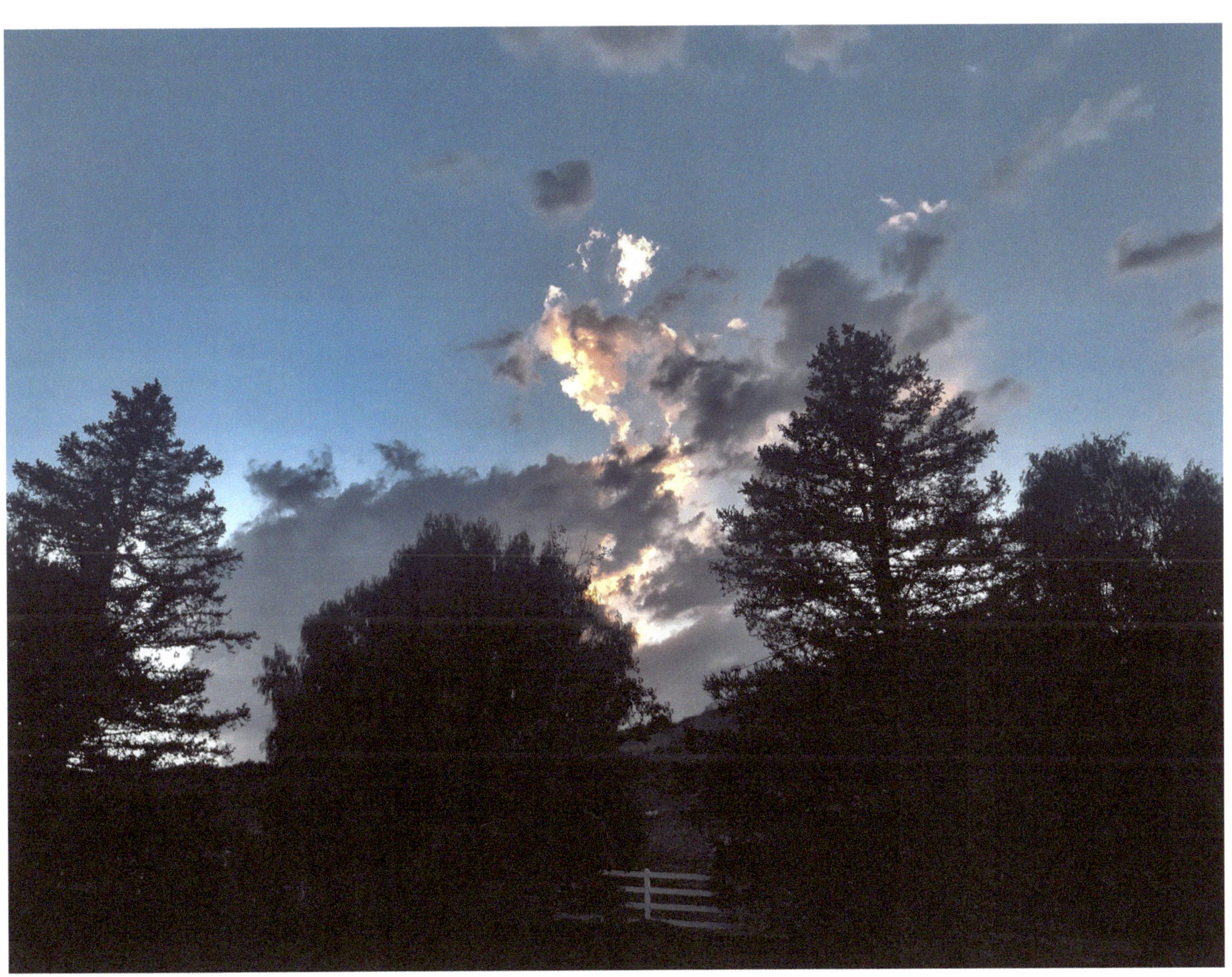

HONOR your father and your mother, that

your days may be long upon the LAND

which the LORD your GOD is giving you.

—Exodus 20:12

Go therefore and make DISCIPLES of all the

nations, BAPTIZING them in the name of the

FATHER, and of the SON, and of the HOLY

SPIRIT.

—Matthew 28:19

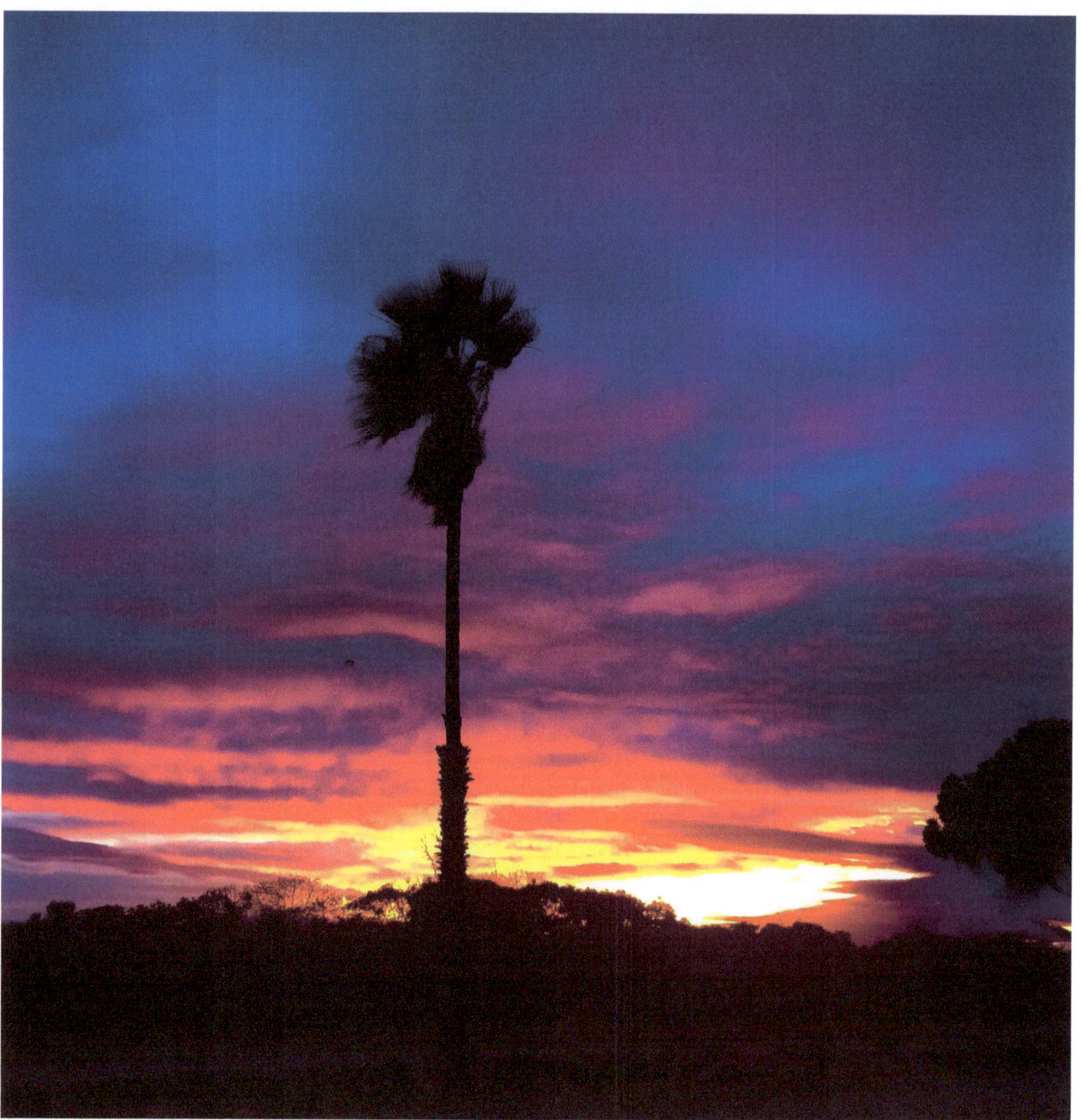

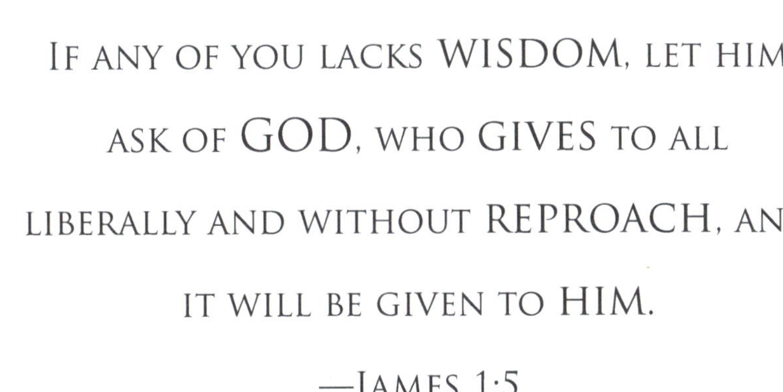

If any of you lacks WISDOM, let him
ask of GOD, who GIVES to all
liberally and without REPROACH, and
it will be given to HIM.

—James 1:5

These things I have SPOKEN to you, that in ME
you may have PEACE.
In the world you will have TRIBULATION,
but be of GOOD cheer,
I have overcome the WORLD.

—John 16:33

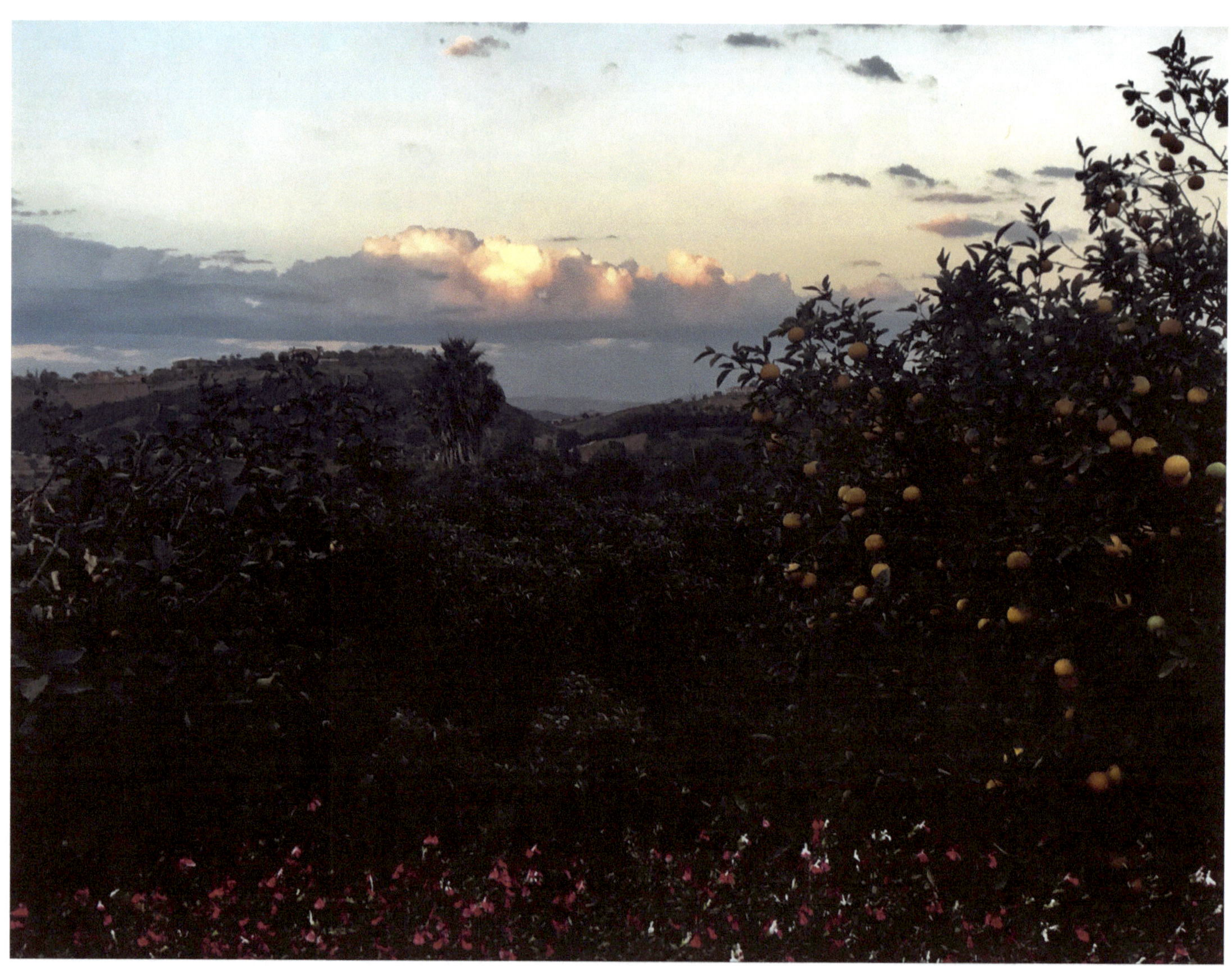

Fear not, for I *am* with YOU;

Be not DISMAYED, for I *am* your GOD.

I will STRENGTHEN you,

Yes, I will HELP you,

I will uphold you with MY righteous HAND.

—Isaiah 41:10

Then JESUS spoke to them again,

saying, "I am the LIGHT of the world. He

who follows ME shall not walk in

DARKNESS, but have the light of LIFE."

—John 8:12

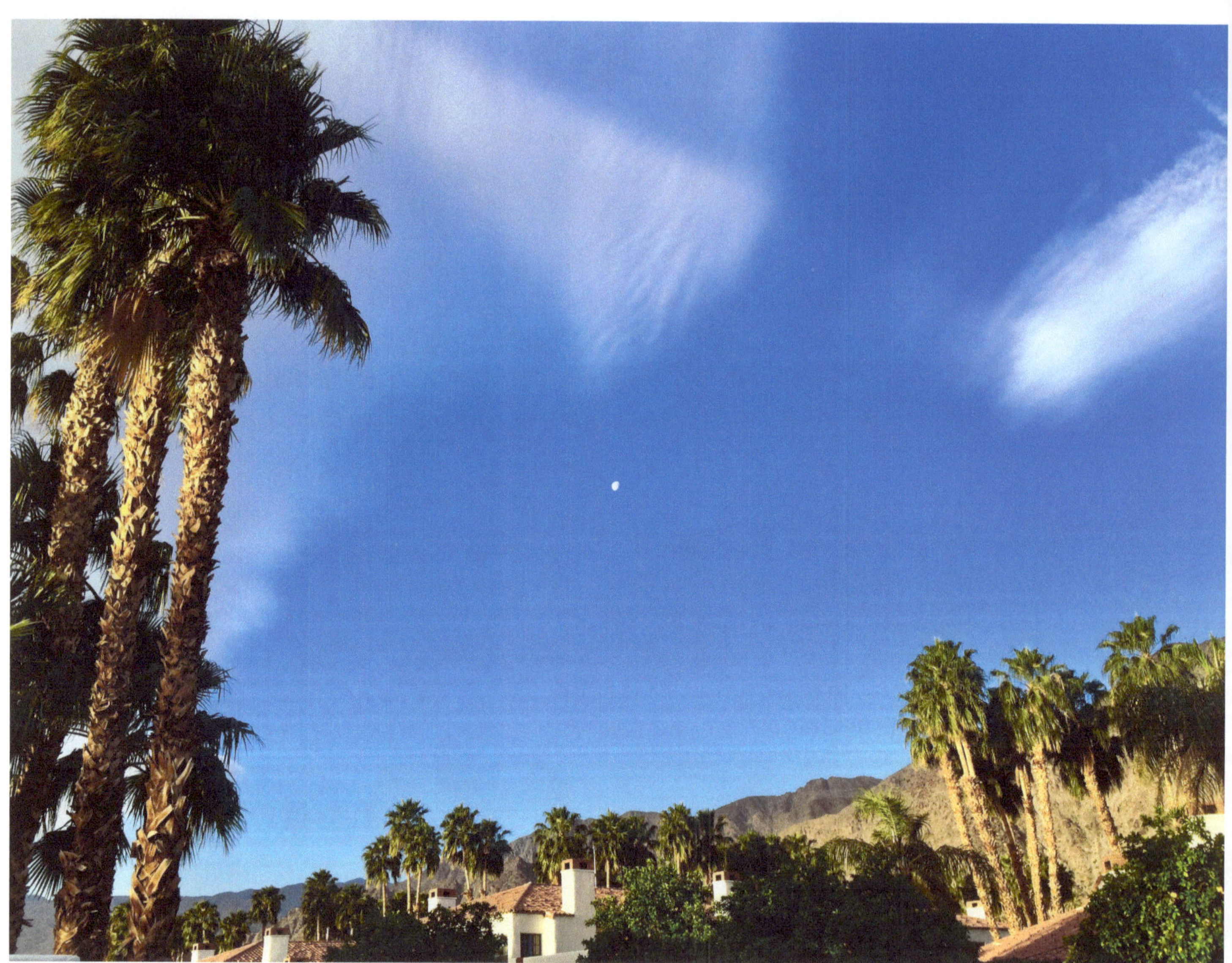

I am with you ALWAYS, even to the end of the

AGE.

—Matthew 28:20

GOD is my STRENGTH and power,

And HE makes my way PERFECT.

—2 Samuel 22:33

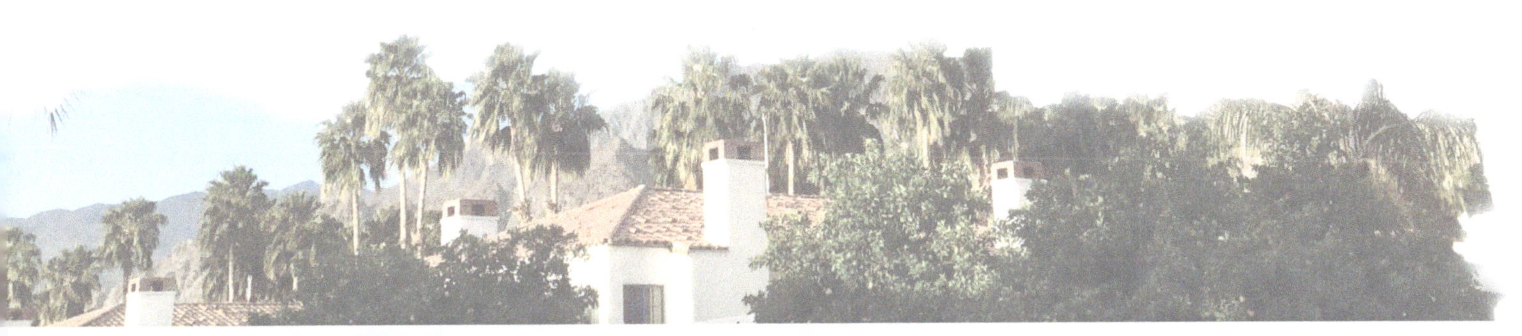

ANXIETY IN THE HEART OF MAN CAUSES

DEPRESSION,

BUT A GOOD WORD MAKES IT GLAD.

—Proverbs 12:25

BEHOLD, *I* STAND AT THE DOOR AND KNOCK.

IF ANYONE HEARS MY VOICE AND OPENS THE

DOOR, I WILL COME IN TO HIM AND DINE WITH

HIM, AND HE WITH ME.

—Revelation 3:20

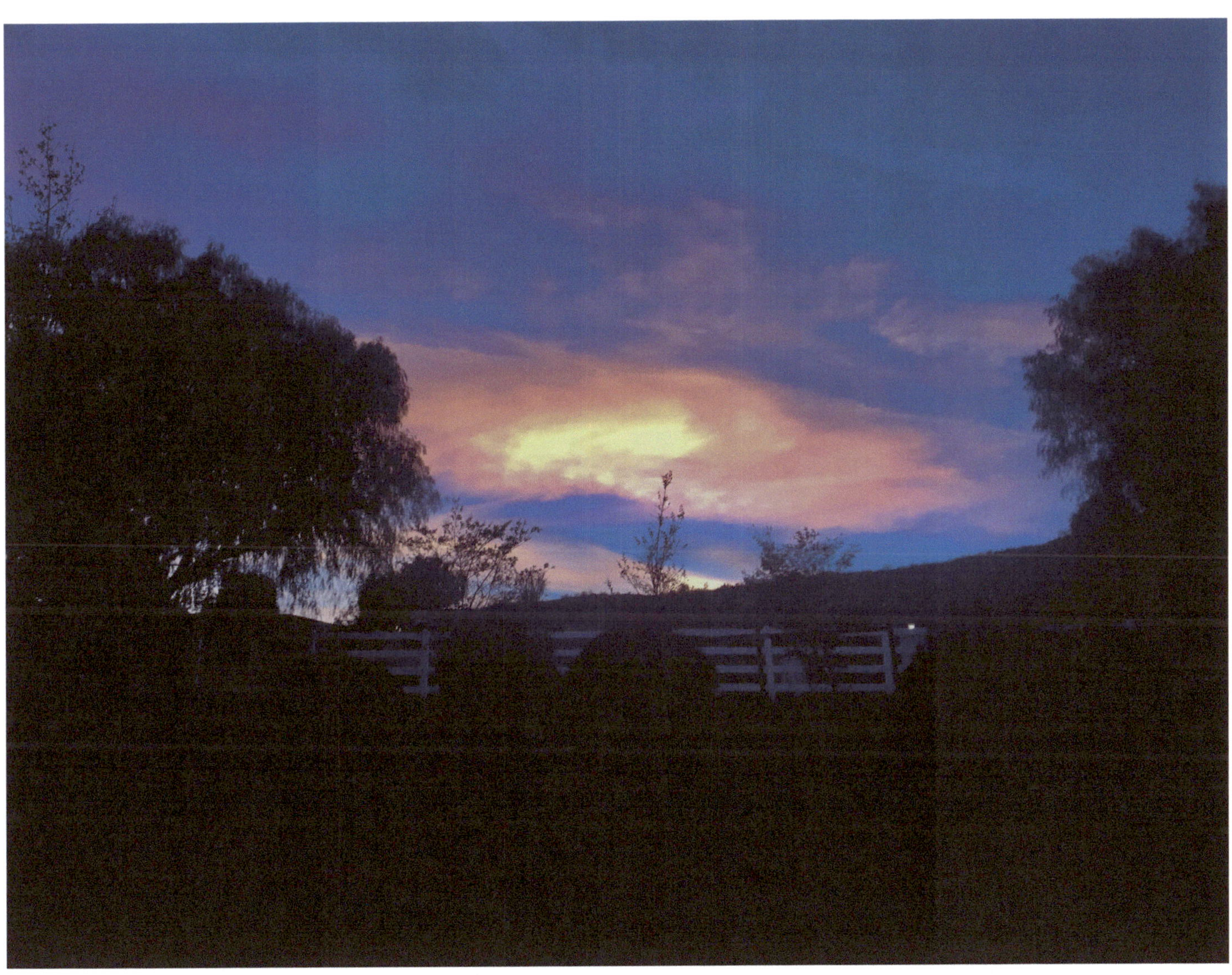

If you keep MY COMMANDMENTS, you will abide in
MY LOVE, just as I have kept MY FATHER'S
commandments and abide HIS love.

—John 15:10

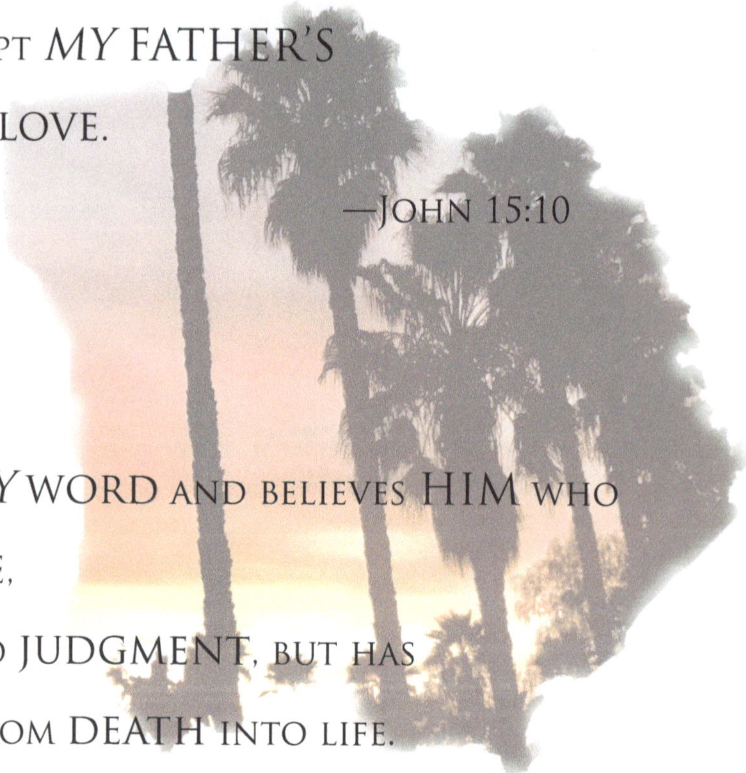

Most assuredly, I say to you,
he who hears MY WORD and believes HIM who
sent ME has everlasting LIFE,
and shall not come into JUDGMENT, but has
passed from DEATH into life.

—John 5:24

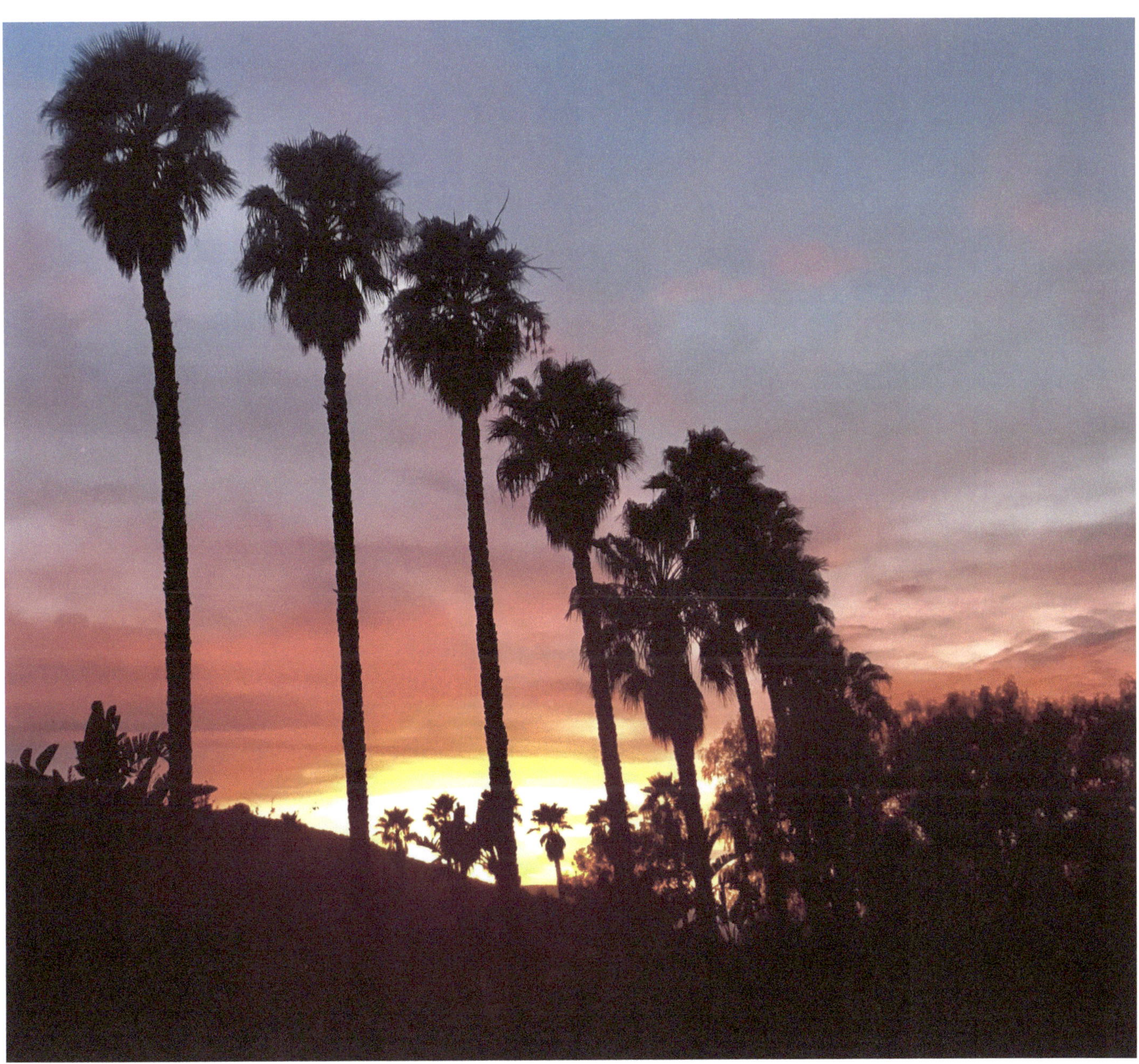

FOR I KNOW the thoughts that I think toward you,

says the LORD, thoughts of PEACE and not of

evil, to give you a FUTURE and a hope.

—JEREMIAH 29:11

SO JESUS said to them, "Because of your

UNBELIEF; for assuredly, I say to you, if you have

faith as a mustard SEED, you will say to this

mountain, 'Move from here to there,' and it will

move; and nothing will be IMPOSSIBLE for you."

—MATTHEW 17:20

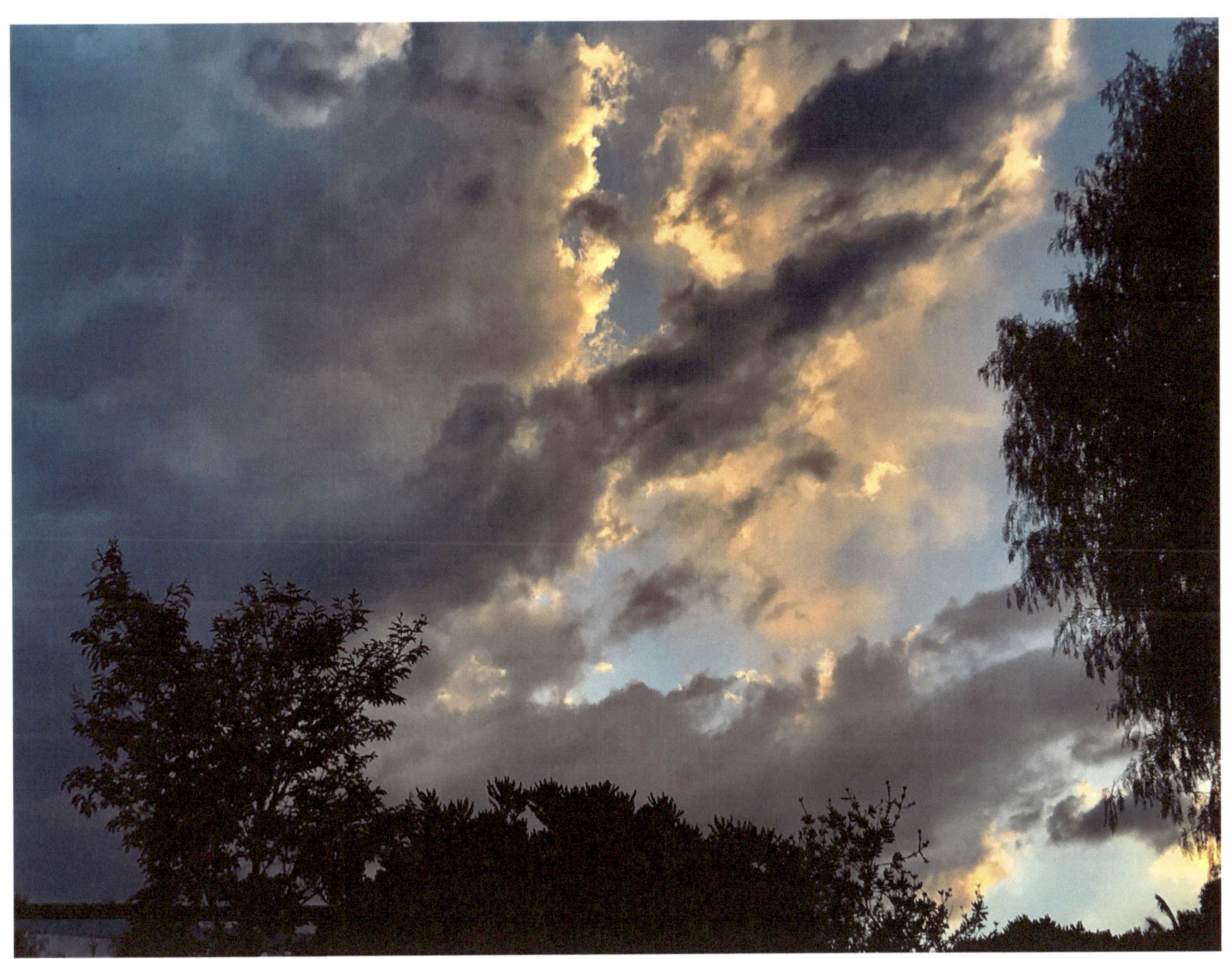

This is the DAY which the LORD has made; let us REJOICE and be glad in it.

—Psalms 118:24

Be CAREFUL how you think; your life is shaped by your THOUGHTS.

—Proverbs 4:23

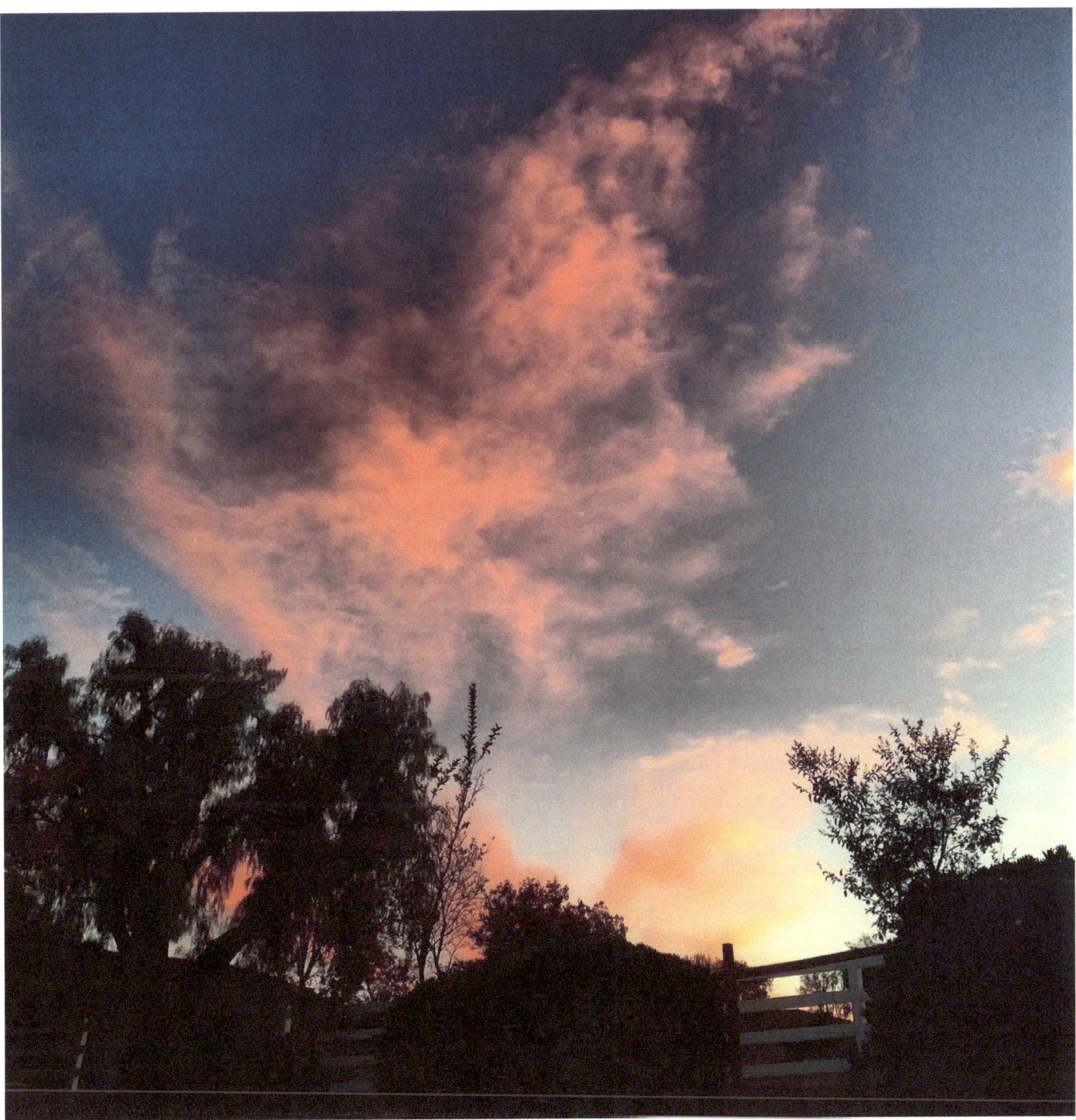

YOUR WORD is a LAMP to guide my feet

and a LIGHT for my path.

—Psalm 119:105

Encourage one another and BUILD

each other UP.

—1 Thessalonians 5:11

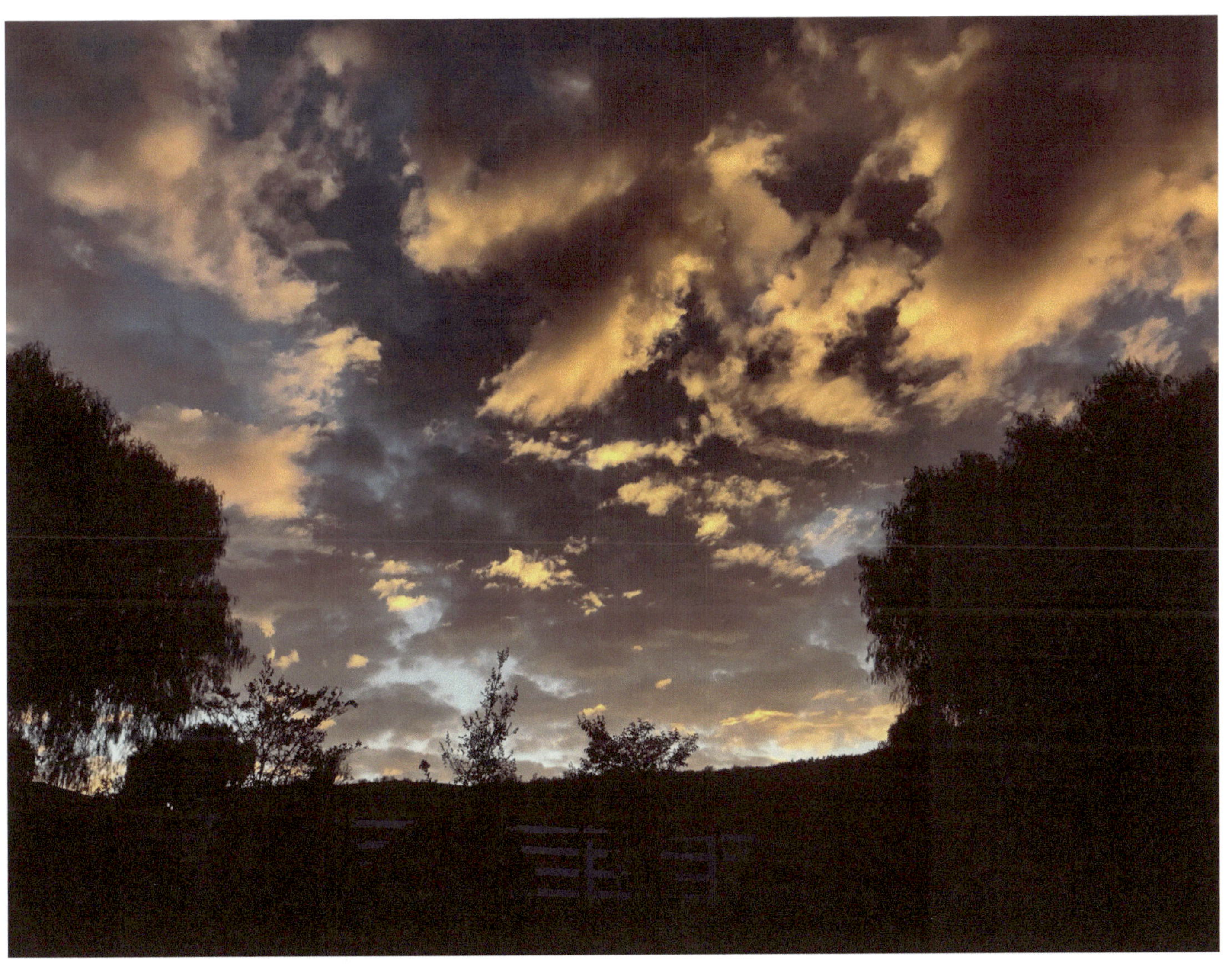

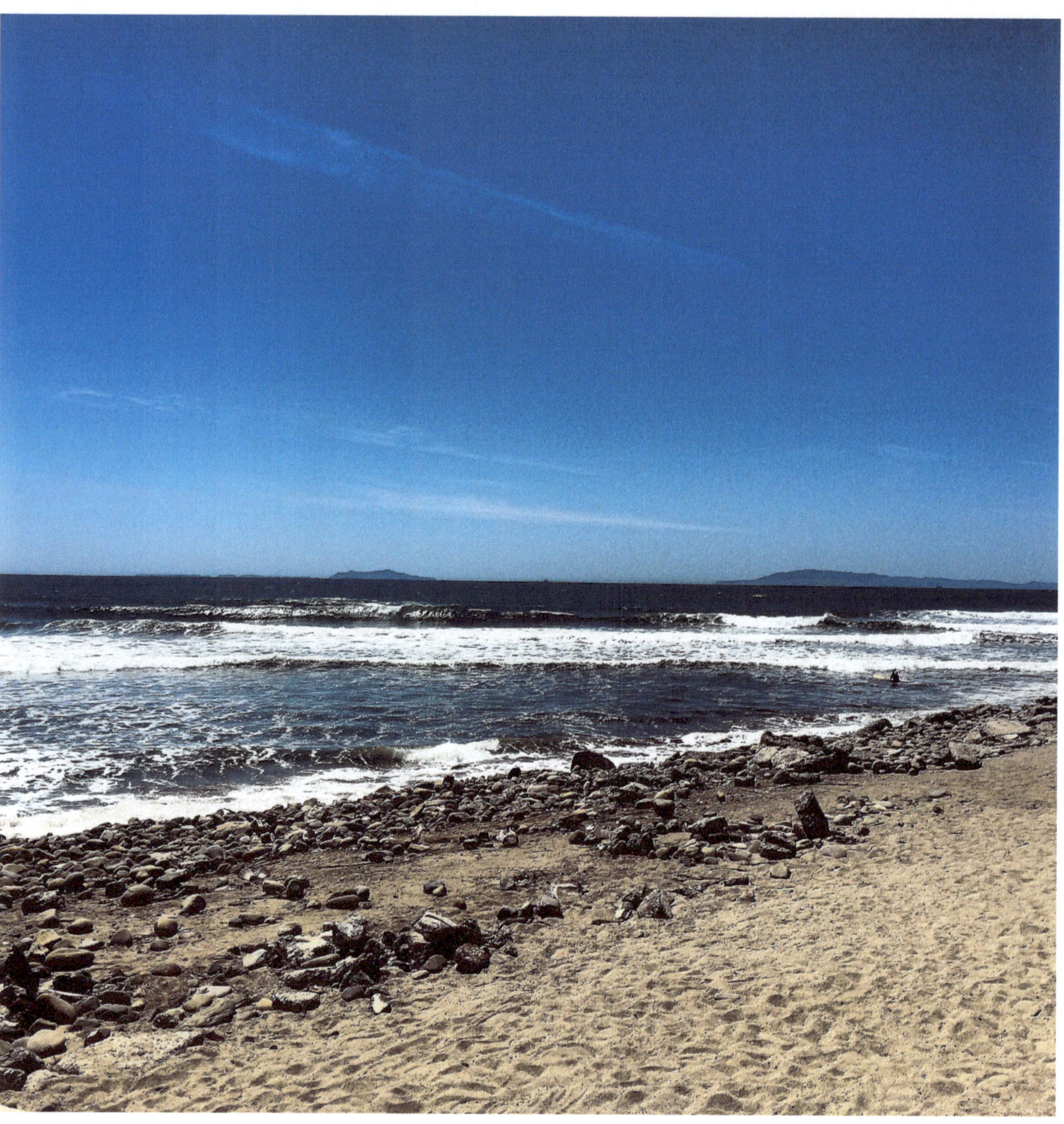

A FRIEND LOVES AT ALL TIMES,

AND A BROTHER IS BORN FOR ADVERSITY.

—Proverbs 17:17

BE JOYFUL IN HOPE,

PATIENT IN AFFLICTION,

FAITHFUL IN PRAYER.

—Romans 12:12

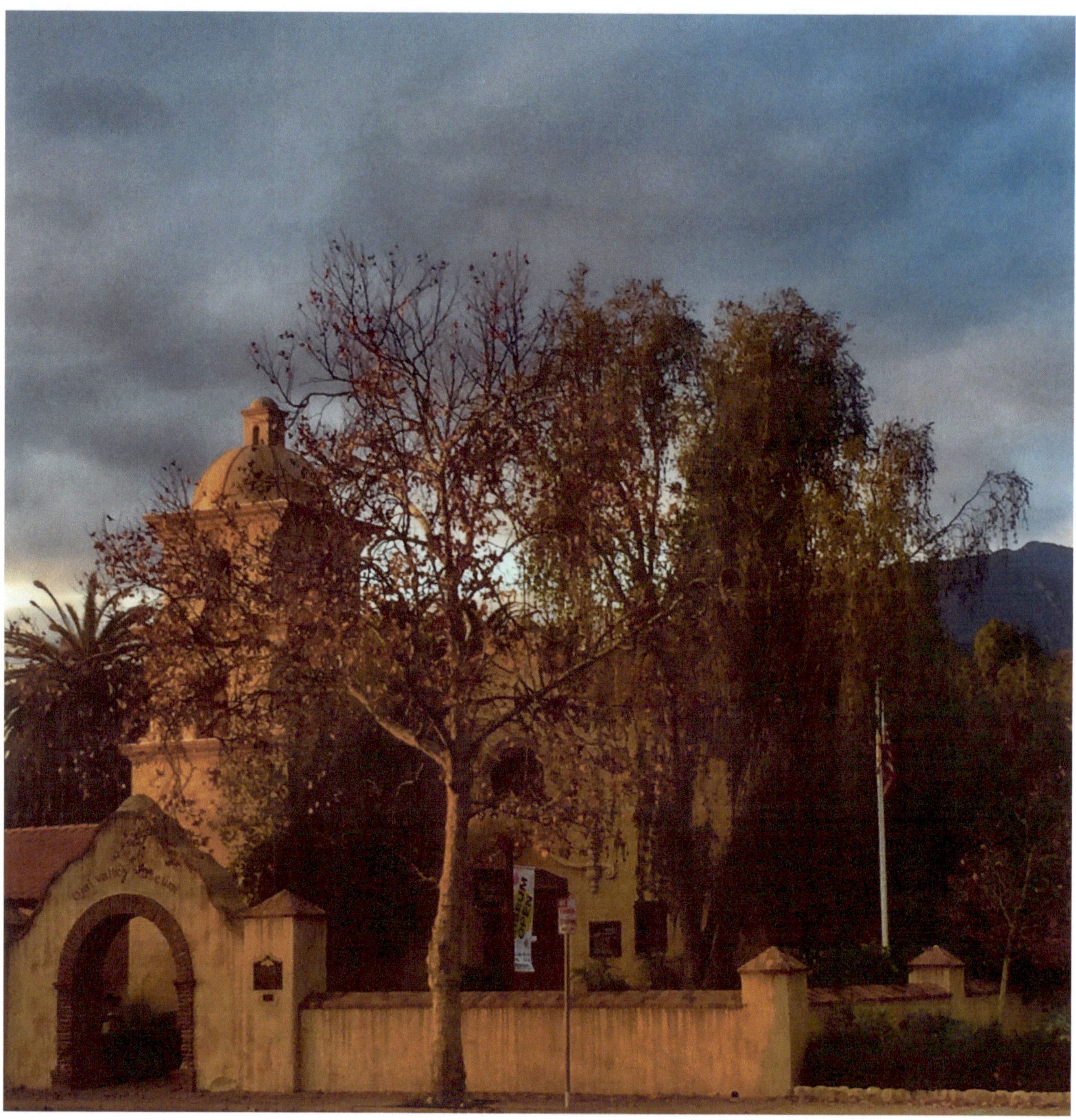
Ojai Valley Museum
MUSEUM OPEN

Let your light shine before men, that

they may see your good works and

glorify your FATHER in heaven.

—Matthew 5:16

Even though I walk

through the valley of the shadow of death,

I fear no evil,

for YOU are with me;

YOUR ROD and YOUR STAFF,

they comfort me.

—Psalm 23:4

Love is PATIENT,

Love is kind.

It does not ENVY,

It does not boast,

It is not proud.

It does not DISHONOR others,

It is not self-seeking,

It is not easily angered,

It keeps no records of WRONGS.

Love does NOT delight in evil

But rejoices with the TRUTH.

It always protects,

ALWAYS trusts,

Always hopes,

Always PERSEVERES.

LOVE never fails.

—1 Corinthians 13:4-8

You shall LOVE the LORD your GOD with ALL your heart, with all your SOUL, and with all your strength.

—Deuteronomy 6:5

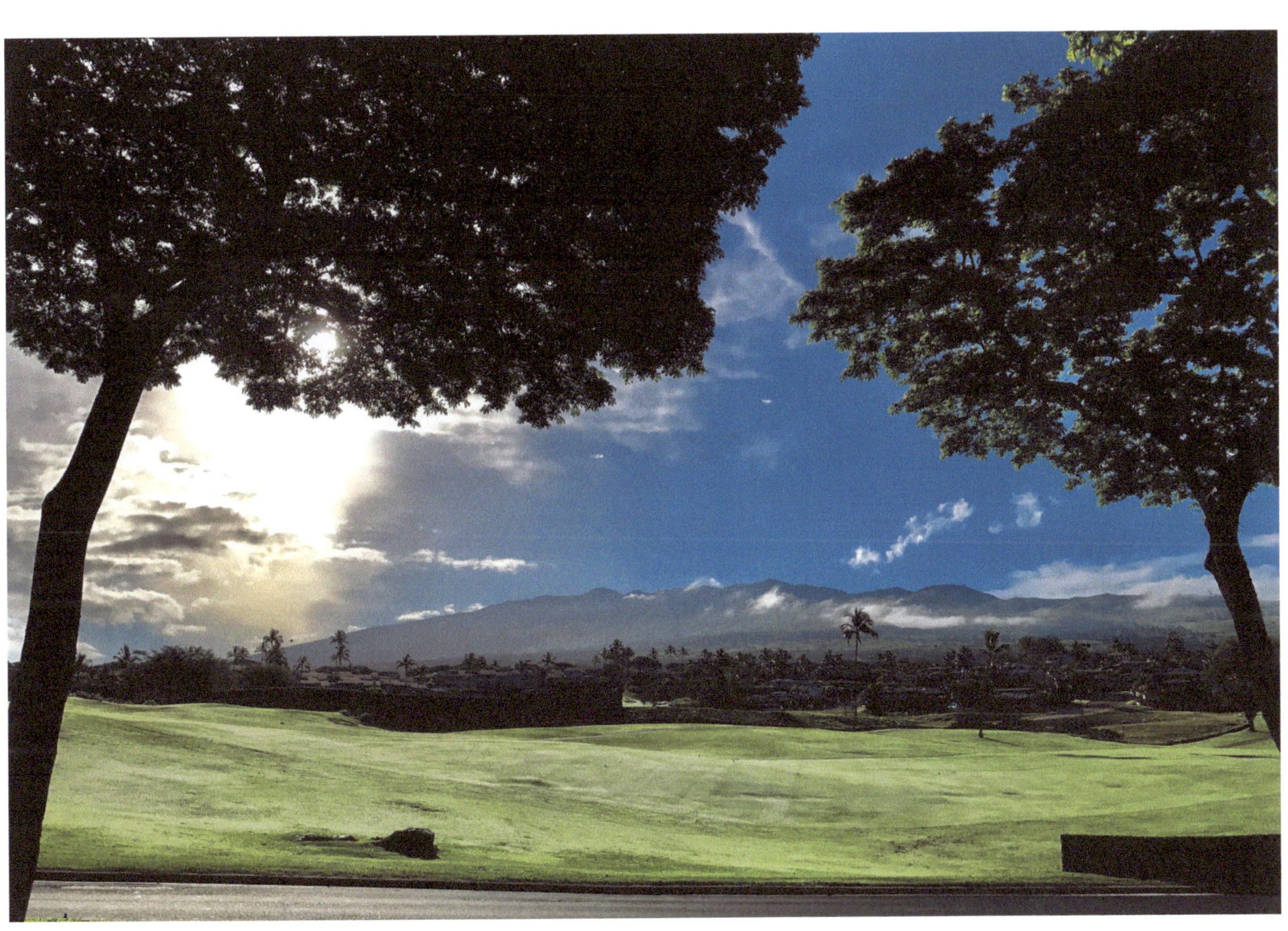

www.ingramcontent.com/pod-product-compliance
Lightning Source LLC
Chambersburg PA
CBHW042202030726
47602CB00007B/97